AN EARLY WORK
LATE IN LIFE

The Art and Life
of DANNY ALLEN

BILL WHITING

Design and layout: Denison Creative, Rochester NY
Printing: pixelPRESERVE, Rochester NY

www.anearlyworklateinlife.com

Cover and title page art:
*Danny Allen, SUNNY DUCKS, acrylic on board. 5 3/16 inches x 3 7/16 inches.
Collection of the Memorial Art Gallery of the University of Rochester.*

This book is dedicated to the Allen family,
as well as to Eva Weiss, Nancy Rosin, and
Kathy Calderwood for helping me remember
the past; to Sarah Gerin for helping me believe
in the future; to Gary Clinton and Don Millinger,
without whom nothing in my life would be
possible; to Gail Lavin for letting me cry in
her office; and to Josef Johns for the inspired
pursuit of simply being Josef Johns.

Above and beyond all, this book is dedicated with
all my love to the memory of Daniel Arthur Allen.

Danny Allen, untitled. India ink and watercolor. Collection of Antonio Petracca.

Eva Weiss, photo of Danny Allen, right, and Ramon Martinez.
Collection of Susan Plunkett.

BILL WHITING 1972

BILL WHITING 2013

CONTENTS

DANIEL ARTHUR ALLEN, 1946-1974

*This photo of Danny Allen wearing his "thinking cap" is
by noted photographer Eva Weiss, ca. 1973.*

In the late 1960s and early 1970s, we believed
we were living in modern times. There were
no cell phones; they hadn't been invented yet.
People didn't have home computers. Of course
there were cars and television sets, but not
everyone had them. America had put a man on
the moon, and we thought we were a part of the
future. Every generation believes they're living
in modern times, and at that conscious moment,
they are. Remember: the past was once the future,
and the present passes with the blink of an eye.

Danny Allen was an unusually gifted artist. He
committed suicide in early November of 1974,
at the age of 28. My writing is a tribute in loving
memory to a wonderful, quirky young man from
a different era.

This book tells the story of the life that Danny
Allen and I shared during the hippie years.
I hope it will also serve as both an archive of
Danny's artwork and a celebration of a life that
ended tragically and all too soon.

BILL WHITING, MARCH 2013

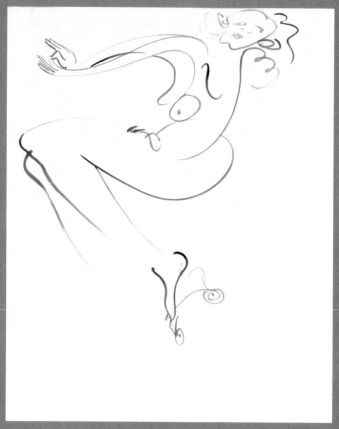

Danny Allen, Lady on Skates,
India ink, 1973.
Collection of Ruth Cohen.

ACKNOWLEDGMENTS

I am very grateful to my inspired editor, Janet Benton, for her insight and understanding of the creative mind. I could never have organized my thoughts without her. I'm also indebted to Katherine Denison not only for her excellent design of this book, but for her encouragement and belief in this project from its very inception. Many thanks are also in order to Andy Patilla for kindly photographing so much of Danny's art. A special thank you goes out to Danny's old friend Greg Walker for all his recollections and technological advice. Thank you to Robert Silver, Esq. for his professional legal advice, and to Christine Long for sharing her memories and connecting me to Thom Akeman, who sorely deserves my gratitude for his kindness and courage.

Thank you to Gerrie and Duck and to the kind people who have graciously allowed me to reproduce art from their personal collections, starting with the Allen family, especially Danny's mother, Bernice Allen; Dan's siblings, Christine Allen Wheat, Jacquelyn Allen-Davis, and Leon James Allen; and Leon's wife, Joyce Naffziger. Thank you to Eva Weiss, Nancy Rosin, Antonio Petracca, Don Millinger and Gary Clinton, Robert Henning and Brian Stenfors, John Grace and Nelson Baldo, Josef Johns and Richard Reisom, R. James Cromwell, Susan Plunkett, Steve Carpenter, Larry Repass, and Stephen Plunkett. Special last-minute thanks are due to Albert Robbins, Ruth Cohen, Wendy Lippman, and Leah Warnick for providing additional examples of Danny Allen's art so graciously at the eleventh hour.

— CONTINUED

I would be remiss if I didn't thank all my many friends whom I pestered into reading various drafts. Thank you to Pat Circolo, Stu Bykofsky, Ruth Reber, Ellen Coupey, Mark Powell, Kevin Kimbrell, Deb Regan, Stephanie Eggar, Diane Ricci, Glenn Hauler, Rebecca Schulman, Michael Brisson, Martha Peech, Robert Sullivan, Tim Barton, Joe Barbella, and Deb and Greg Mayro.

The book itself is an acknowledgement of Danny Allen, who is gone but not forgotten. Also gone but not forgotten are Dan's and my friends Ramon Martinez and David Lortz, as well as Diana Wilber, who is now institutionalized, suffering from severe aphasia.

I would likely be gone also, if were it not for the help of a great many supportive friends. I feel the need to single out a long overdue thank you to Tom Vogt for helping to pack up my things and drive me to my new home in Philadelphia many long years ago. You might just have saved my life.

Danny Allen,
Conté crayon on newsprint.
Collection of Ruth Cohen.

Danny Allen,
tiny graphite drawing, 1972.
Collection of Eva Weiss.

I WAS BORN AND RAISED in the white-bread, fiercely Republican town of Moorestown, New Jersey, the second son of conservative and overly protective parents. When I departed for college in 1968, I was an uptight kid. No one had ever taken the time to sit me down and teach me the facts of life or the ways of the world. I'd heard things only from other kids, not all of which were entirely accurate. And my most pressing worry was that I would fail at a seemingly insurmountable challenge. I knew I must never let anyone know my deepest personal secret: I was a homosexual.

I had, through no choice of my own, grown up to become the very sort of person my parents had warned me about. I'm reasonably certain, upon looking back, that everyone who knew me already suspected I was gay, but people didn't talk openly about things like that in my snooty hometown. The sexual revolution was in full swing, but I was only marginally aware of it. In fact, nothing was ever discussed in any depth in my WASPy home. Subjects were talked around. Anything controversial or potentially unpleasant was addressed only with an exasperated facial expression and sealed with silence.

But I've never ascribed to the constraints of being a WASP. Unlike the rest of the family, I've always been an emotional person. But I was ill prepared, once on my own, to understand what it meant to fall in love and to cope with the complexities of having another person in my life. And I haven't needed an onion to water my eyes since receiving a forwarded email that has set my memory of those times in motion. Memories rarely shared with anyone have launched me on a bittersweet spiritual journey into the past.

Almost forty years after the death of the great love of my life, an unexpected email arrived out of nowhere, like a letter delivered decades late from a dead soldier to his widow. The part of my past it addressed has never been far from my mind, and my clumsy way of meeting life's challenges has come back to haunt me during sleepless nights, when I ruminate over minor infractions or accidental slights. I've never wanted to hurt anyone, but it's inevitable in this life that everyone at some time will hurt or perceive themselves as hurting someone, albeit unintentionally. When I do sleep, I dream, often about the unwise paths I've taken and where they've led me.

There are many things I've done that I regret. With regard to one of them, I would say in my defense that it's not wise for parents to launch a child out on his or her own with only a sunshine-and-lollipops understanding of the world. I was so completely naïve about matters of the flesh that—secretly knowing I was homosexual—I thought my semen could not impregnate my college girlfriend. But biology has a mind of its own. My vehemently anti-abortion mother loaned me money to pay for my girlfriend's abortion. My father was never told. And such are the communication skills of upper-crust white people in lockjawed old East Coast communities.

I mention this calamity to reveal the degree of innocence with which I was launched into the world. The aforementioned email, however, wasn't a late birth announcement telling me I had a child who'd already passed his or her fortieth birthday (although I have wondered in moments of reflective paranoia whether my college sweetheart did or did not go through with the abortion; we were kept apart). Instead, the email was an inquiry about a tiny painting located in a museum's storage room in Rochester, New York. The message had been forwarded to me like a hot potato by a dear friend. She hadn't wanted to stir up old pain, but I was the sole person to whom she could logically turn. Information was needed about that tiny painting and the artist who'd painted it, and I had those answers.

I'm now in my sixties, and the painting in question, although long out of my sight, remains very dear to me, not just for its imaginative beauty, but also because of who painted it. I am an artist myself, but the painting bears no mark or assistance from my hand. I like to think I'm a good artist, although there's every reason to believe I'm merely an accomplished hack. There are so many people in this world whose art is vastly superior to my own, which is not to say that I create bad art, only that I'm wise enough to know that judgments about the quality of art are made by juries of people who might not yet be born. There's a randomness to what survives in this world and what becomes discovered—and by whom. This random process defines the art of the past. Yet with this email, I was given the chance to rescue a small place in history for a certain artist from my own past. Here is the message received by my old friend Kathy Calderwood. Knowing the long-buried feelings it would stir up, she forwarded this to me:

> Dear Kathy Calderwood,
>
> I am a student at the University of Rochester, doing research for the Memorial Art Gallery's permanent collection. I came across a wonderful painting by Daniel A. Allen entitled **Sunny Ducks**. So far I have not found much information on the piece. However, in the file was an appraisal you had written, and I was wondering if you have any information about Daniel Allen or the piece itself. Any information would be extremely helpful! I find this piece fascinating and would love to know more about it. Thank you so much for your time.
>
> Sincerely,
> Sarah Gerin

The new attention to this piece may not go down in the annals of art history as would the resurfacing of a lost Vermeer, but in my heart and mind, both he and it already hold such a place. And no one else had the information I did about its maker. I have kept and protected Danny Allen's artwork for decades, and there's so much more art and correspondence to locate, not to mention so many things to scan, either from slides or from an old portfolio case that the email got me to reopen after many years in which it remained sealed, stored in the dark, out of sight, but never lost or forgotten. A short reply could never make sense of Danny Allen or his tiny little jewel of a painting. I sent Sarah a detailed message, of which the following is an excerpt:

> *Hi, Sarah,*
>
> *Before I begin, I want to thank you for noticing and appreciating Danny Allen's painting* **Sunny Ducks**. *I'm an older gay man. Danny Allen was my lover when we were young. He committed suicide in early November of 1974 at age 28. He was and remains the one great love of my life.*

I remember his painting, **Sunny Ducks**, *to be very tiny—only about 4 x 6 inches, or maybe 7 inches—it's hard to recall after all this time. Dan used layers of glazes and tints to build up surface subtleties in color and tone—often using a triple-zero sable brush and floating colors between finely, almost French-polished layers of varnish.*

Danny sat in on lectures and workshops in the Art Department at Rochester Institute of Technology—smuggled in as a nonpaying student. Some of the instructors knew and turned a blind eye. Other professors were too high on pot to notice or care. It was a different, experimental time back then. Nevertheless, Dan was better than any of the paying students. He had incredible talent, but deciding to be any kind of an artist isn't setting up a guarantee, no matter how gifted one is, for recognition or easy entrée into the art world. Today, as a painter, I still use techniques I picked up from watching Dan intuitively at work.

There's more to tell than I could ever cover in one email. Dan killed himself while I was in Toronto on business. He jumped off the Driving Park Bridge into a narrow section of the Genesee River, where off season it becomes a glacial gorge of rocks with a trickle of water. He took his life in early November, before the winter snows give way to the spring thaw.

The Rochester Memorial Art Gallery holds an annual juried show called the Finger Lakes Exhibition, where artists and craftspeople from Rochester and vicinity compete for placement in the museum's main gallery. I entered Danny's little painting, posthumously on his behalf. The late pop-realist painter Lowell Nesbitt juried the show. Mr. Nesbitt selected Dan's painting to be included in the exhibition. After the show came down, the painting was accepted for the permanent collection as a gift in Dan's memory.

I hope this long-winded diatribe was helpful. There's so much more that remains only in my heart and my head. Until now, I didn't know if anyone other than old mutual friends would ever care to know or ask about Danny. Thank you so much for asking and for seeing what I have always seen in Danny's work.

My best to you,
Bill Whiting

Although I didn't know it at the time, Dan's wondrous little painting would eventually be included in a show of rarely seen artworks from the museum's vault. Dan's work was once again going to see the light of day.

Danny Allen, watercolor of Bill Whiting, ca. 1970.
Collection of WTW.

After sending this email, all I could do was think about Dan and reflect on my early days of living on my own. My memories were helped along by looking at the artworks I have of Dan's.

Once he talked me into taking off all my clothes and going naked into Lake Ontario with him while we were picnicking with our peculiar friend Diana Wilber. Dan did a little watercolor of me standing knee-deep by the water's edge. I had long, auburn hair at the time, and while I'd posed nude once for another artist in the college dorm, I'd never intentionally stripped naked outside, where just anyone could see me. It was the first time I'd allowed myself to be so free, but this freedom came naturally to Dan. The sketch doesn't look like me so much as it relates the spirit of the moment. But he has captured the way my eyes squint when my glasses are off, my pale reddish coloring, and the prudish posture I took on while revealing myself. Dan could see right through me.

Danny, among other heartbreaks and calamities, was what I'd tried to leave behind when I moved to Philadelphia in 1977. Yet over the passing years, I learned that I couldn't leave heartbreaks behind merely by relocating to another city. Painful memories pack themselves up like stowaways in a hidden place in your heart, only to unpack themselves and revisit you when they're good and ready.

Sarah Gerin had no way of knowing the floodgates she'd opened by way of her inquiry. Our correspondence has remained ongoing, and my thoughts keep traveling back to the hippie daze, when my friends and I were viewed askance by straight-laced people, much the same way punks, Goths, and new-wave youth have been viewed by starch-brained, unimaginative people in recent years. The hippies and the beatniks were the forerunners of today's social and cultural rebels. Those of us who remain might look stodgy and old to younger eyes, but they'd be surprised to learn how well some of us tired older folk know them, without so much as exchanging a word.

In the spirit of the surreal, dream-like quality of my late lover's art, I think it only right to relate a reoccurring dream that visits me without warning.

A building floats in the air. It's a stone structure, perhaps a palace. Its exact form changes from one dream to the next, but there's an abstract understanding that it's always the same building. Sometimes the building floats on a vast expanse of still water, with the horizon stretching all the way to infinity. But most of the time, this mysterious facade hovers in the sky, a structure anchored to nothing at all but in no way unstable. It's fixed and motionless, solid architecture residing within its own confines in space. The mysterious floating building is surrounded only by a perfectly blue sky in which clouds continually change form, suggesting shapes as they dissolve into one configuration or another, as does any good sky.

After years of being visited by this dream, I found myself permitted to enter the building. I have no idea how I found myself inside; I was simply there. The building revealed itself to contain only one large, spacious room, a place with a purpose, carved from marble or alabaster, with story-high, opened windows giving way to views of clouds that pass by with the breeze. It's an important room, grand while elegant in its simplicity. Walls hung with silks in everchanging hues rise from polished stone wainscot to a massive cornice that defines the edge of what should be a ceiling. In place of a ceiling, my eye finds only the open sky.

I know instinctively that the stone beneath my feet is solid, safe, and stable, even as the room hovers somewhere between nowhere and stillness. I sense, without being told, that if I were to exit through one of the arched openings, I would float and tumble without any control, entering an endless state of free-fall.

I'm not the only person in the room. Men and women pass outward through the arched openings, but they don't fall. The visitors fade in from a mist when entering the room and dissolve into vapor as they leave. They are a variety of ages, all neatly dressed, serious, dignified, making their way through the chamber, taking no notice of me.

People walk up to various sections of the walls to inspect elaborately framed artworks, magnetically drawn from one picture to the next. The walls are filled with art, hung salon-style, magnificent paintings that defy description and change before my eyes from portraits to landscapes to images I'm unable to describe. I observe as visitors stop to inspect the pictures that catch them. When they're satisfied with what they have seen, they leave, dissolving into the outdoor sky.

I am unable to leave. I cannot walk through the archways without risking my own free-fall. The other people are different from me. I'm flesh and blood, while they are somehow able to merge with the mist.

I walk over to a man with a gray mustache—always the same older gentleman in a dark suit. I ask him where I am and why I'm there. He tells me that I'm at an exhibit of all the artworks Danny Allen would have created had he chosen to live. And I'm suddenly in free-fall.

I wake up, startled, and shake what I've dreamt out of my head, trying to understand whether the experience was real or unreal. For a moment I'm dazed, caught between asleep and awake. What I carry away from this dream is an ethereal message: that I must create something I can show for myself every single day of my life in order to justify being alive.

I am commanded to create and to do nothing less. But no matter what I do, it will never be enough, or good enough. I suspect I'm not the only artist who's felt this way.

Danny Allen,
Moi, *self-portrait in India ink, ca. 1970.*
Collection of the Allen family.

Danny Allen, shadowbox assemblage, mixed media, ca. 1970.
Collection of Wendy Lippman.

THE PATH OF ANY PARTICULAR person's life cannot be that individual's alone. Quirky, peculiar characters were the norm in the stoned-out art world of the late 1960s and early 1970s, and I remember them as I remember Danny and our Rochester life. Eccentricity had to be pretty far-out before anyone would be considered beyond the pale.

A bizarre cast of characters had begun parading through my life well before I met Danny Allen. I was living off campus in a large, second-floor apartment. The building was in a row of white clapboard townhouses on Rochester's Washington Street. I'd had a variety of roommates, including a stripper who fed white mice to a boa constrictor she used as a dance partner on stage. Then, later, a sweet and gentle Native American man named Dwain, who told me stories about Danny long before I'd met the man. Since Dwain wasn't the first person to tell me about Danny, his stories further reinforced the fact that everyone in the world knew this mysterious Danny Allen but me.

After Dwain moved out, an effeminate roommate—no, make that an androgynous, screaming queen named Jimmy—took his place. One night, Jimmy came back blind drunk in the wee hours of the morning, having mistakenly picked up an equally inebriated butch lesbian on the street. I was awakened by a piercing scream from the bedroom down the hall. Jimmy and his street pickup had just discovered that they each possessed completely different sexual apparatuses from what they'd led themselves to expect. The shockwaves hit them when they both realized they were poised to engage in an unintentional act of heterosexuality.

I got a glimpse of her as she ran out. Granted, she did have sideburns. But Jimmy always wore too much bronzer and a full face of make-up. He really did look like a girl in bar light, especially with his permed, strawberry-blond Afro. After I saw Danny's surreal watercolors, I came to think of this communications failure between star-crossed gender-benders as a real-life enactment of Dan's gender-blurring watercolors, so many of which I have kept safe in darkened storage for decades. Of course Jimmy had known Danny Allen years before, having hung out with him in San Francisco. In Jimmy's estimation, just knowing Danny Allen, even tangentially, gave him bragging rights.

Danny Allen,
watercolor, 1973.
Collection of WTW.

Before I'd met Danny, my neighbor Diana Wilber was the person who made the strongest claims that Danny Allen would become my lover. If she mentioned it once, she harped on it a thousand times, claiming that she was "much better acquainted with the future than the past."

Diana professed her own eternal love for Danny Allen with florid, nearly silent-film-star gestures. It warrants mentioning that Diana was prone to quaint displays of drama. Sadly, she is now in a nursing home, stricken with Alzheimer's disease, which is distressing in and of itself. Also distressing is the fact that, while I was staying with her shortly after Dan died, Diana pinched all of Danny Allen's writings and poetry from a leather binder I'd

kept tucked in my belongings. I discovered they were gone and asked if she
had taken them, but she denied it while giggling in her devilish way. This does
make it ominously unlikely that a sizable number of Dan's poems and art will
ever resurface, for there were drawings tucked in with those writings, and
Diana had also accepted artwork from Dan in lieu of rent over the years when
he'd come and gone from her life.

Diana kept a townhouse two doors down from where I lived. She decorated
her walls with Indian-print bedspreads and filled the house with antiques,
art, and a clutter of books and curiosities. During the hippie years, Diana was
what can best be described as an earth mother. She was rather heavyset, with
a very pretty face. Picture Mama Cass crossed with a full-figured Mona Lisa.
Diana worked with no small measure of success at being odd. For example, she
communicated with me largely through a string of non sequiturs or by blink-
ing at me in Morse code, expecting somehow that I would understand her. I
rarely knew what the devil she was talking about. She'd be burning incense
and meditating in the front parlor when suddenly she'd burst out with odd
sounds like "KAH-ROO!" Diana was perfectly capable of being lucid, but being
peculiar was the persona she'd chosen as her brand.

Dan had lived as a boarder in Diana's apartment, sleeping on a cot in the basement and working upstairs, wherever there was enough light to lavish detail on
his intricate, miniature graphite drawings. This is how she had come to know
him so well. But he wasn't the only person she'd helped along while bating her
snares. Diana's apartment was always open to artists and writers, serving as a
Rochester home base for fascinating people, each of whom had a mysterious
history with Diana. She was constantly preparing hearty soups and stews in
the kitchen, with an extra place set for whoever might happen to stop by. For
all her peculiarities, no one could accuse Diana of lacking hospitality. As I was
the new art student on the street, Diana would frequently feed me dinner. At
nearly every meal we shared, somehow she'd work into the conversation how
Danny Allen was coming back and that he would be my lover.

When only the two of us were having dinner together, she might become
peevish, making me feel as if she wanted me to leave. But when I'd offer to
go, she'd start pleading with me to stay, even dragging after me, tugging at
my shirttails. Diana required patience and a fine appreciation of the absurd,

but I was willing to put up with an awful lot to get a good meal. And Diana was a damned good cook. I was too skinny, having shed far more weight than was healthy after I'd left home for college. In her own way, Diana was looking after me. Often I felt that I was a stand-in for Danny Allen, a substitute until he came back home to her. There was something magnetic about Diana, but magnets can sometimes be difficult to pull apart. Eventually I'd make my way home, far later into the evening than I'd intended, still needing to do my course assignments for studio critiques.

Then one day I finally met Danny Allen. It happened on the front steps of Diana's apartment, on one of those rare warm and sunny days in Rochester. Eva Weiss and her then-lover Leah were there in front of the house, too, dressed like pirates because that was their style. (Come to think of it, I'm sure it was Eva who introduced me to Diana, setting the whole chain of events in motion.) I thought instantly that Dan was attractive, although he also looked sort of exhausted. I could sense right away that he was plotting to get me naked, and I had every intention of letting him.

Dan was wearing dark glasses, but I didn't realize at the time why. It turned out that he had hepatitis and had come home to Rochester so Diana could look after him. He'd been sick for a while, but still he'd chosen to hitch a ride across the country, from San Francisco to the East Coast. Not the best way of dealing with a serious illness, but Dan did things his own way.

His illness allowed me to get to know him before we hopped into bed—not the way things were normally done during the uninhibited days of the sexual revolution. So Dan and I fell in love before we ever made love. I'd stop by and visit him pretty much every day while he recuperated. To protect me from getting sick, he'd have me roll a joint and smoke half myself, then hand over the remainder to him. One of the first things I remember him saying to me was, "I won't be able to have sex with you until the doctors tell me I'm well enough." I thought his comment was both terribly forward and oddly erotic, even kind of romantic.

When I visited Danny at Diana's, he'd show me his portfolio, which humbled me. His work was far more inventive and individualized than my own. And he wanted to know more about me, which made me kind of self-conscious.

I wasn't accustomed to anyone wanting to know more about me while sending unmistakable signals that I was attractive. It was a flattering yet unfamiliar sensation.

Dan asked me about my work, but almost all of what I had was at the studio at school, so there was very little to show him. Instead I related a story about a figure-drawing critique I'd recently experienced. My instructor had never liked the fact that other students came to me rather than him to ask how to draw a foreshortened limb or to achieve a sense of proportion. My figure drawings, even my quick sketches, showed a faithfulness to the figure that my classmates admired. During one studio assignment, the class was allowed the luxury of working on a prolonged pose over the course of three sessions. I had done a tightly rendered but dispassionate drawing, anatomically correct to a fault. My drawing style was academic, and I knew it. My classmates had watched my progress and had admired my rendering. When time was called, we were told to pin our work up on the wall, and each piece was critiqued in an open exchange. When my turn came, the rest of the class liked what I had done and said so, but the instructor was less than enthusiastic.

I told Danny, "The teacher took my drawing down off the wall, threw it onto the floor, and in front of the entire class, he ordered me to walk on it."

"Did you do it?" Danny asked.

"No," I replied. "I walked out of the class."

Danny laughed. "I know that instructor. He's an ass, but he didn't do you any harm. I think in his own tactless way, he was telling you that your piece lacked individual interpretation. He probably felt it was too tight and correct, like a photograph, not offering any personal insight into the figure. More than likely he isn't capable of doing a drawing as good as yours, which is the flip side of the coin." I pondered his points as he continued. "But you still haven't answered my question. What is it that you most enjoy doing as an artist?"

I told him that at one time I'd wanted to be an architect and how some of my favorite childhood memories were of creating models and building miniature houses. Dan replied, "You should build one now, as an adult. Take something like that into a studio crit! It would totally freak out your instructors. They wouldn't have any frame of reference for it."

It had never occurred to me to do something like that. I wasn't entirely sure if my instructors would even consider it to be art. What Dan was trying to tell me was to feel passionate about what I was creating, and "to the devil" with what anyone else thought of it. What mattered was how I felt about the art I took the time to create.

While entering this flirtatious friendship with Dan, I felt like we had known each other all our lives. It was a feeling something akin to indigestion, only it was exhilarating. Trying to make sense of this feeling, I could reach only one conclusion: I was falling in love.

After a period of chaste visits centered on discussions about creativity, I came to see Dan after a painting class. He had pre-rolled joints in his pocket, as well as the news that the doctor had given him a clean bill of health. He lit a joint and inhaled, then exhaled it directly into my mouth. Dan kissed me for the first time with pot smoke and was undressing me before I could even figure out what was happening. I was with a man who seemed far worldlier than me— an active, practiced player in the sexual revolution. Danny had also just spent a prolonged and uncustomary period observing celibacy. There's no need for lurid details, but we christened the daybed in Diana's den while she was out of the house. The details of that memory belong to me.

Although at first this remained unspoken, it was clear from the beginning that Danny and I were a couple, just as Diana had predicted. But Diana, for all her ebullient generosity, had a meddlesome streak. Once Dan and I started actually seeing one another—in spite of the fact that she had predicted it—I was cast in her eyes as her rival for Danny's affection.

For every wonderful and generous thing Diana had to offer, along with the bargain came Diana herself.

She was known to dress up like a witch or a lady wizard, complete with a pointy, cylindrical hat and robes decorated with moons and stars. She'd wear this getup while riding around town on a miniature motorbike that was dwarfed beneath her magical robes, which fluttered behind her in the wind. Diana claimed to have powers, and in fact she did—but not the kind she boasted of. She knew how to get under your skin and convince you she knew something you had yet to learn.

She also had the power to mess herself up. It was not at all uncommon for Diana to make shallow cuts in her wrists—not deep enough to do real damage, but deep enough to allow her to make bloody snow angels on the front lawn in wintertime. These performances would award her with the attention she craved, along with a trip to the emergency room, where the attending physician would pronounce her perfectly fine and she'd be summarily discharged. Diana described episodes of this sort as her only way of letting Danny know how much she was in love with him. Her behavior could be very trying, yet she was such a compelling, manipulative character that we were at a loss to do anything other than tune in for her next round of histrionics. Besides, she fed us both almost nightly.

Danny Allen, watercolor, ca. 1970. Collection of WTW.

Diana had a short, checkered career working at several animal-testing laboratories, each time staying just long enough to gain the staff's trust and a set of keys or combinations—at which point she would liberate all of the animals, including the rats, and move on to the next clinic, until all the clinics for miles had her blacklisted.

I never thought Diana would ever find another job after that, but somehow she managed to get hired by a hospital. I don't know how or when she found the time to work. She seemed to always be poking her nose into other people's business and hanging around when you least expected her. Diana was a relatively young woman, but she didn't seem to have an age, and she didn't seem invested in any sort of career. She merely WAS, and we accepted her as such.

We all had a particular fondness for Diana's cat, Pweedwyn. Pweedwyn was a child's pronunciation of the word *penguin*. Somewhere, there are drawings that Danny did of the poor, cockeyed creature, but who in the world knows where they are? Prior to Diana liberating him from a research facility, the poor thing had been partially lobotomized, or something of the sort. The animal's eyes were never quite looking in the same direction; they were locked in a split gaze, with each eye going toward an opposite end of the room. And the cat's behavior didn't exactly reveal a great intellect. Pweedwyn would climb up on a kitchen chair, make his way to the windowsill, step onto the kitchen counter, and walk across the sink so he could curl up on top of the stove for a warm, winter's nap. A short while later, his tail would be on fire from the pilot light, and he'd jump to the floor, hissing and screeching, only to repeat the same routine over and over again, to Diana's endless amusement. Diana did not own a television set.

Diana was a study in contradictions. She liked saving animals but was inured to the need to protect them from themselves, her cat being the most obvious example. She also liked collecting people and tormenting them into being beholden to her. When Danny first arrived, he stayed with Diana, but he'd lived with Diana before and been suffocated by her need for attention.

Soon after, I found myself at a crossroads. All of my roommates had either VW-bussed-it to San Francisco or moved on to strip palaces in other cities. The lease was up, and I couldn't afford the apartment alone. Danny had no money. So I moved one street over to a place that we could afford that was within my budget: a magic little Victorian garden apartment on Greenwood Street.

Dan Allen in Diana's parlor.
Photo by Eva Weiss.

My memory is graying at the temples, but I can still see the place clearly in my mind's eye. We'd landed an apartment with a tiny carriage house folded into the bargain rent. My parents were willing to foot the bill during my final year of college, so Danny and I lived there for free. The apartment had an odd layout. We entered through a side door into the kitchen. To the right was a funny little room that could be used as either a living room or an extra bedroom. It collected furniture and other objects but was fundamentally useless, because it was out of the traffic flow of the apartment. We decorated the room with curb picks and hung our art on the walls.

To the left of the kitchen was a good-sized, rustic shed that we used for our bedroom. It was a drafty room, but that made it all the better for cuddling. The room had a peaked, open-beamed ceiling and a second row of exposed stretcher-beams, which had probably once supported an attic floor on the half-story above. It was like a tall log cabin, and in it we placed a high-backed, golden oak Victorian headboard, which watched over us when we made love or slept. Victorian furniture hadn't yet come back into favor, so we found amazing things for next to nothing in junk stores or on the curb. We had objects that would probably have genuine value today. I sold them all before moving down to Philadelphia.

Our rustic, romantic bedroom had a secret back door that opened onto a tiny brick garden path. The path led to the side entrance of our carriage-house art studio. It was a brave little building with an attitude of its own, vaguely favoring the north, courageously leaning into the Canadian winds that blew over Lake Ontario and dumped ridiculous amounts of snow on Rochester, Buffalo, and Syracuse. The last time I saw the carriage house was during a visit north to Rochester about twenty years ago. Someone had meticulously restored it into a tiny jewel-box of a private home. That made me very, very happy.

Both Dan and I were prolific and creative in that wonderful little carriage house. I imagine that it has magic in it still. It certainly did during the countless hours Danny and I shared together, listening to a transistor radio, absorbed in our respective projects. That carriage house holds the best memories of my life—because there is nothing in this world like new love when it's your first. But new love doesn't last forever. A person survives this life by remembering the better experiences, the finest moments shared with family and friends. Those recollections carry us through the days when sadness and loss visit our solitude. When you venture into the darkness, intent on confronting troubling memories, you begin a risky journey, yet one that can yield valuable lessons once you unlock what you've kept boxed up in a secret place in your soul. Those memories are there for a specific purpose: to percolate wisdom for use later in life.

Danny Allen, detail from The Visitor *series, India ink on bond, 1972. Collection of WTW.*

Back then, I had not yet percolated enough accumulated life experience to have wisdom, so I overlooked or underestimated the obvious: Danny had demons. You could see them in his art, if you chose to look for them. He had dark humor, too, sometimes intentional and sometimes through pure happenstance. But just because two people live under one roof doesn't mean they're both sharing the same experiences.

I returned from shopping downtown one day, entered our apartment, and knew immediately that something was wrong. I'd walked in on Danny doing himself harm. I found him standing in our bedroom, gasping and choking. He'd tied a pair of ladies' pantyhose tightly around his neck, apparently having draped both stocking legs over a low ceiling beam, then stood on a chair and kicked it out from under himself. The pantyhose stretched all the way to the floor, however, leaving Dan with both feet planted firmly on the ground. He was perfectly safe—but unable to free himself, tethered within a very limited range, and gasping for air. I cut him down with kitchen shears. He was more embarrassed than anything else.

I held him tightly in my arms, rocking him back and forth, telling him never to do anything like that ever again. I asked him why he would try such a thing in the first place. All he said was, "I'm depressed." No further explanation. He assured me that his depression wasn't caused by anything I'd done, but I found it impossible not to internalize. Moods like sudden storms came and went with Dan; while I was holding him, he started to laugh and cry simultaneously, and finally he was laughing so hard at the predicament he'd created that I joined in, until neither of us could stop. At the time, I didn't grasp the undercurrent slicing through that dark, comic act. To me, his ill-conceived attempt at suicide was just another stunt, like Diana and her bloody-fucking-fake snow angels. But it was not.

We were living together, engaged in a delicate balancing act, positioned somewhere between black comedy and disturbing reality—all of which was blunted by smoking pot and the distractions of sex. Dan and I were coming from very different places, viewing life from polar-opposite extremes, without knowing how to discuss our differences. I didn't understand what was happening with him, nor did I know what was really going on in life in general. Simply put, I knew nothing whatsoever in my early twenties. Who does?

I recently received a letter from Nancy Rosin, an old friend of Dan's and mine. Also an artist, Nancy was one of Dan's work partners; they shared fourhanded freelance projects. She shared a recollection from those times in her letter: "We were sitting around in Diana Wilber's house one evening, months before Danny died. Danny was 'entertaining' all of us with a very funny story about trying to kill himself by sticking his head in an oven. I remember all of us laughing, and then Diana cackling at him, 'Danny, you don't really want to kill yourself. If you really wanted to kill yourself, you'd go jump off a bridge!'" I don't recall having been present for that exchange of prophecy, but the story didn't surprise me. Dan and I lived on different but parallel planes, with me avoiding life by building dollhouses and Danny willing to blow up the apartment while trying to inhale gas fumes.

It's entirely possible that I might have been in love all alone. To this day, I'll never know. I thought we were setting up a household like any other couple, following the heterosexual model, which was the only model I'd known. But Dan was approaching our being together from a very different place. In fact, even though we were lovers, he felt perfectly free to have sexual encounters outside the relationship.

I first discovered that Dan had outside dalliances when we accompanied each other to the public-health clinic for penicillin to cure the clap. Later, I nursed him for a prolonged period while he recovered from a relapse of hepatitis. I eventually had to move him back to Diana's house for a temporary stay because her apartment wasn't as drafty as our little place. (For some reason, I tested negative for hepatitis.) Diana was in hog heaven, having the upper hand over Danny's care as he recuperated on her living-room sofa. Diana turned out to be just the tonic Dan needed; she drove him so crazy that he forced himself to feel well enough to come back to the carriage house and our apartment. We were together again in the studio, making art. That turn of events launched Diana into another one of her delusional three-way love-triangles, embellished with her own brand of imaginary romance, espoused to anyone who would listen.

I took care of Danny through later STD episodes, including Giardia-lamblia, which he'd contracted from an old "friend-with-benefits" who'd blown into town after serving in the Peace Corps. Then there was impetigo—who knows where that came from. And of course there was generic gonorrhea. I didn't yet know myself well enough to realize that I possessed a caretaker's personality. I'd been raised that way, groomed for the part. While not very happy about it, I dutifully took all these developments in my stride, as best I could—even when the incidents I learned of hurt me deeply.

Back then, during the widespread freedom of newly liberated gay promiscuity, we were—or at least Dan was—knee-deep in temptation. The mood was one of "free love"—smokin' doobies, crankin' up the stereo, and goin' with the flow. I remember Danny laughing and telling me that I'd been born "inherently uncool." I had to get with the program. But perhaps that really wasn't what he wanted.

It wasn't until much later when he asked me if we could have an official open relationship. When a man asks for an open relationship, he isn't really expecting his other half to take him up on it. It's always conceived of as a one-sided proposition, which means it's not particularly well thought out. Generally, this sort of a thing never works very well for anyone—at least in my experience. But that comes later in my story.

Danny Allen, nonobjective painting, acrylic, ca. 1968.
Private collection.

Danny Allen, Bunny Lady on a Cherry Pie, *acrylic with suspension glazes, 1974. Collection of Susan Pluckett.*

ROCHESTER'S CORNHILL DISTRICT, where Dan and I lived, retained the good bones and extraordinary charm of its earlier opulence. The city's boom times began in 1825, when the Erie Canal linked Rochester and other population centers to the prime trade markets of New York City and beyond. Flour became Rochester's biggest export, earning it the nickname Flour Town and transforming Rochester into a wealthy agricultural center. The good fortune continued; in 1889, George Eastman founded Eastman Kodak there, and in 1906, Xerox was established (originally called the Haloid Photographic Company). All of this industry added up to Rochester becoming a recession-proof small city. Sadly, like most American cities that boomed in the nineteenth and early twentieth centuries, Rochester is no longer recession proof.

When Danny and I were living in the apartment with the carriage house in Rochester's once-fashionable Cornhill District, the borough was a bit down at the mouth. The wealthy had moved decades before to the comparative safety of upscale, suburban towns like Pittsford and Brighton, leaving their heritage behind to decay. Yet the late 1960s and early 1970s saw our community moving into a state of transition from ghetto to gentrification.

This process was hindered by an ill-advised urban-renewal project of the 1950s that spawned the I-490 corridor, cutting a swath right through the center of Rochester. The damage was done by well-intentioned city planners, who demolished the earliest part of the historic district, leveling some of the finest examples of nineteenth-century architecture in America. Thus our immediate neighborhood was split in two, like twin cities, dotted with grand antique homes on either side of a multi-lane highway. The city had always been divided, having been built along both sides of the banks of the Genesee River, linked by the Court Street Bridge. But the fanciest houses had the river views, and most of them were gone, replaced by a heavily trafficked highway.

The wealth of the earlier era had led to some wonderfully eccentric architecture. Some of the houses looked like columned Greek temples, while others were exotic Victorian mansions decorated with bracketed cornices, decorative brickwork, and magical towers. All were intriguing leftovers from a prosperous past.

During the period of gentrification, we saw an odd mix of players in the neighborhood. Nouveau-riche investors were restoring Victorian jewel boxes to their original grandeur in the midst of ghetto blocks filled with low-income housing projects, hippie art students, and whorehouses. I recall a wild, no-nonsense black woman named Delores who ran a house of ill repute around the corner from our apartment, where drunken patrons tumbled out of windows or were tossed onto the street, arms and legs akimbo, while loud music blared out every window. After the long Rochester winters passed, giving way to brief periods of warm spring and summer weather, loud music filled the air at all hours. We'd hear a cacophony of rock, folk, and jazz blaring out of apartments occupied by hip artists, writers, and musicians. I always recall those days when I hear Eric Clapton's classic song "Layla." The whole neighborhood had a wonderful aura of shabby grandeur and the hope of new beginnings.

Dan and I lived not far from Jenny Churchill's family home. She was the American-born mother of England's legendary prime minister. On the other side of the highway stood exotic mansions, such as the Moorish-style Brewster Burke House, where the front porch and tower looked like they belonged on top of a decorated East Indian elephant rather than on the facade of a house. Several blocks away, early feminist suffragette Susan B. Anthony had made Rochester her home base. Against this rich backdrop of history, decay, renewal, and hippie lifestyle, Danny and I made ourselves at home, too.

According to Nancy Rosin, she and Danny played a part in saving the old Victorians of the Cornhill District. Before Danny went to San Francisco, Nancy lived in a battered, rundown Victorian house on Troop Street, which cozied up to Greenwood Street. Out of nowhere, she got an eviction notice telling her that the landlord was knocking down the old Victorian to put up an office building. Danny, Nancy, and a motley group of protestors took Nancy's landlord to court to get a stay on the house's demolition. Nancy described an unlikely alliance:

little-old-lady historic preservationists, led by the Daughters of the American Revolution, were rubbing elbows with hippie freaks and conceptual artists, who were cheered along by the generic college rabble-rousers who attended all protests, regardless of the cause, faithfully high on something or other.

A petition was circulating to designate Cornhill as a national historic district. Preparations were made on both sides of the controversy. A date was set for a hearing over the fate of Nancy's home, with a precedent-setting landmark ruling at stake. According to Nancy, on the day of the hearing, a large contingent of artists calling themselves the Gallucci Family (as if they were connected to the mob) descended on the courthouse. None did so as conspicuously as one Daniel Arthur Allen. Danny was wearing bell-bottom trousers and a shirt with feathers sewn all over it. Around his ankles, neck, and wrists were East Indian jingle bells that pierced the courtroom silence with the subtlety of shattering glass. Whenever Dan shifted his weight, the room would tingle with the sound of tinkling bells.

While the case was still in litigation, a bulldozer started itself up, or so the official story goes, and plowed directly into the old Victorian house that the preservationists were trying to save. The demolition was purportedly blamed on ghetto kids who found the keys in the ignition and started up the bulldozer. But there were no witnesses and no reasons to believe that story. The battle to save Nancy's house was lost, but the war was won. Cornhill was rezoned as a protected historical district.

Flash forward several years to my college graduation. My parents came to visit in order to witness my graduation ceremony and realized I was gay and living with a lover; thus our financial gravy train came to a screeching halt. I had to get a job. My good friend and drinking buddy Larry Repass allowed me to inherit his old job, which he was vacating so he could move to New York. So I began to work at a Lane Bryant branch store, which specialized in clothes for large and tall women. I was expected to be a one-man display department for the only store in town catering to the full-figured gal. I had no idea what I was doing.

*Danny Allen, pencil sketch
of Larry Repass, 1970.
Collection of Larry Repass.*

*It's curious how some of
Dan's work is signed "Nada,"
like this example.*

But we needed to pay the rent and to eat, so I taught myself how to dress a mannequin. There were no big-girl mannequins back then, so I had to neatly roll the backs of the clothes into French twists and pin them in place so they would fit the slender mannequins. I'd walk outside to see if any of the hidden yardage showed from the street. Sometimes I hired Danny to assist me in making window sets and backdrops. I also got him temporary work painting some of the store's interiors.

While at Lane Bryant, Dan and I met a wonderful, stylish, and hilariously funny young woman named Adele Fico. Adele, in her natural generosity, connected us to a variety of fascinating people who opened up our world. During the day, Adele worked in a department she referred to as Junior Jumbo Petites. On evenings and weekends, we danced, drank, hung out, and generally got into mischief, with Adele clattering from place to place in her chunky platform shoes. She knew everyone, and if she didn't know them, they knew her. If you've ever known anyone who was capable of reading from the telephone directory word for word and making you laugh out loud with every utterance, that was Adele. She's the sort of person whose very name brings a smile to your heart.

Danny Allen, mixed media and graphite, 1974.
From the collection of Robert Henning
and Brian D. Stenfors.

Although Adele's friendship with me has endured the years, the job at Lane Bryant did not. On a Sunday afternoon when the store was closed, Danny and I set out to repaint that very same Junior Jumbo Petites department. The store was empty, and the manager, Mr. Kirshner, was out of town on business. Danny persuaded me that we had to make love on Mr. Kirshner's leather-topped mahogany desk in the executive office. Dan could talk me into anything.

Unfortunately, Mr. Kirshner arrived back early from his business trip and stopped by the office on his way home, catching us in the act, full throttle. He watched stoically as we dressed, both of us blushing with contrition. He then stood over us silently, arms folded, while we completed the paint job and cleaned up after ourselves. To the man's credit, he did cut us a final paycheck before showing us the door. Out on the street, Dan and I couldn't stop giggling and broke out into a run. We raced each other home across the Court Street Bridge and back to the apartment on Greenwood Street, where we finished the other project we'd started, eventually falling asleep in each other's arms.

Danny Allen, quick ink sketch, 1973.
Collection of WTW.

I JUST TOOK A BREAK FROM THE PAST TO WALK MY DOG IN THE HERE AND NOW.

I live on the edge of Philadelphia's historic district, with its sedate, Federal-style homes that reflect the still-lingering tone of a long-gone Quaker heritage. When I reached an area only a few blocks away, I heard the magnified beat of Lady Gaga's latest dance hit and watched from the sidelines as a gay-pride festival took place. I didn't take my dog too far into the noisy crowd of gay revelers, although a part of me wanted to.

How Dan would have loved witnessing something like this. Two young women walked by hand in hand, one with purple hair and the other with green, their matching nose rings clinking as they kissed. Also among the crowd were conservative Jesus freaks, who were shaming their messiah by shaking hateful signs that damned anyone who viewed the world differently than them. I could see into tents where young men danced in tight bathing suits, indelible-ink tattoos covering their arms, backs, and chests with images, looking nearly as if they were wearing torn, patterned shirts. In the carnival atmosphere, the dance music took on a tribal quality.

Then a serious-faced youth, studded with piercings, drunkenly knocked into me, mussing his multicolored Mohawk.

"Whadda you lookin' at, Mista?" he asked confrontationally.

"Nothing," I replied. "I was just gazing through you into the past."
For a moment I'd forgotten how old I must look to a man-child of his age.

"Freak," he muttered.

"Yes," I thought, "I suppose he's right."

Danny Allen, Conté crayon on newsprint, 1973.
Collection of WTW.

After losing my job at Lane Bryant, and while I still had nearly shoulder-length hair, I worked at McCurdy's Department Store, first as Christmas seasonal help. Then I left to work at the more prestigious Sibley, Lindsay & Curr, whose penchant for snobbery led to my getting short, slicked-back hair. I jumped to Edward's Department Store when I was offered more money, only to have the store go bankrupt right out from under me, then returned to Sibley's. None of those historic retail establishments still exists. They're probably all Macy's franchises by now. Isn't everything?

During my days of working as a staple-gun queen in various department stores, Dan took piecemeal work—freelancing for interior designers, painting rooms, wallpapering, or doing painted finishes. Occasionally he'd sell his art-work to friends, but mostly he gave it away. A lot of artists are prone to doing that; creative types are not by nature good business people. And everything in our lives back then was about getting past the boring, practical stuff so we could return to the time we shared in the carriage house, making art.

Danny had the northeast corner of our studio, with the light streaming in from the window by his right shoulder. I took the southwest corner by the side door, since my projects were usually larger in scale and that part was more open and spacious. Dan would lavish hours on end on a single piece, getting every detail just right on his tiny, magic-realism paintings, or he'd dash off sketch after sketch in Conté crayon or India ink. Drawings simply fell from his imagination.

Sometimes he talked me into posing nude, but those drawings never seemed to get finished, except in the bedroom. (That isn't to say that our time was spent unwisely; art was being produced.) What surprised me about Dan's nudes was that they weren't necessarily gender specific. I didn't take the vagueness as an insult to my gender, and I don't think I actually looked an-drogynous; sometimes he merely wanted a figure to refer to, and he did with the drawing what he pleased.

One Saturday in early autumn, after we'd been living together well over a year, rumblings in our stomachs told us lunchtime was drawing near. We prepared to stop our work when we heard a ruckus coming from the front of the carriage house. Since our neighborhood was prone to wild, noisy outbursts, I didn't pay this one much mind. But Dan could see what was taking place from his front-facing window. Four little white boys were restraining a little black boy, and all of them appeared to be in the seven-to-nine-year-old range. A fifth white boy was crying and pleading, because the four bullies were trying to make him punch the black child in the face. The little boy didn't want to do it, no matter how much the four tormentors screamed at him.

Danny burst out onto the scene with the authority of an adult and the lingo of the era, shouting, "This is totally uncool!" When Dan declared something to be "cool" or "uncool," no further discussion was necessary.

Startled, the four white bullies ran away, leaving two bewildered little boys looking up at us. They were frightened and wanted us to stay with them until they were sure the other kids had gone. We invited them into our studio so they could calm down and feel safe. On entering, both children looked around with wide-eyed amazement. There were paintings and drawings pinned up on the walls, and one of my giant dollhouse projects dominated the back of the room. Dan asked them what had been going on, but the boys were more intrigued with what was happening in the studio.

Bill Whiting, Cornhill-inspired, Mansard-style dollhouse, ca.1972. Collection of Rosemary Disney.

They told us their names were Scotty and Junior. Scotty was a scruffy little white kid, and Junior was black. They were best friends and often played together. But Scotty's older brother, Bobby, and his gang hated seeing Scotty hanging out with a black kid on the school playground. And when the boys continued playing together on the weekends, Bobby and his gang felt compelled to impose their own version of martial law.

With introductions made and the bullies gone, Dan cleared away some floor space and gave each of the kids a tablet of paper and some crayons so they could entertain themselves while I fixed lunch. The four of us sat on the floor together, eating tuna-fish sandwiches on toasted white bread along with cups of Campbell's Cream of Tomato Soup, buttered Ritz Crackers, and glasses of milk. Junior told me it was the best tuna-fish sandwich he'd ever tasted.

Rain had started to fall, so the four of us stayed in the studio, where the boys colored with crayons and grilled us with endless questions about art, painting, miniature houses, rock music, and why they were being told the world was round when everything looked flat, and on and on and on. Dan patiently answered their questions, laughing at their childish wonder while making it perfectly clear that they could watch him paint or look at the dollhouses, but they weren't to touch anything except the crayons and the tablets he'd given them.

Clearly that didn't quite sink in. They were getting into everything at once, knocking things over and touching miniature furniture they'd been told not to go near. With no lack of charitable intent, I mean to tell you that these were semi-feral children—two decidedly energetic little boys who were dying to make a huge mess everywhere as their inquisitiveness got the best of them. They were clumsily grasping at everything they saw and touching things they'd been told to stay away from in no uncertain terms. Dan took it all with much better humor than I did. I was busy trying to repair the leg of a delicate miniature chair I'd recently carved, gluing the snapped pieces back together. The boys would settle down for a little while, only to get boisterous all over again.

Looking back, I realize that this was probably the most magical day of their young lives. As they waited for the thunder and rain to pass, they got to watch us work in a room filled with creative energy—something so completely different from the "energy" they'd experienced everywhere else in their young lives.

Darkness was falling earlier, now that it was autumn. The sky was dark once the rain stopped, so Dan and I walked Junior and Scotty home. Scotty lived in a dilapidated old wooden house toward the end of our block. His older brother, Bobby, gave us a sneer, looking exactly like the classic bad kid from an *Our Gang* comedy. Bobby was sitting on the lopsided front porch where a stretch of railing had once been, kicking one of his bare feet back and forth and chewing on a weed. From inside, we could hear at least two adults screaming at each other at the top of their lungs. A door slammed as Bobby spit the weed onto the ground, avoiding looking directly at any of us. Scotty, with a visible sense of doom, ran past him into the house.

Junior said he'd be all right getting home. He said he knew how to get home from there. But Dan insisted that we see him home safely. We doubled back around, heading due south, toward a relatively new but decrepit Section-8 housing project that Junior called home. A drunk had collapsed in the doorway of Junior's building, and the man was snarling something into his bottle, directing his mumbled words at no one in particular. People had to step over him as they came or went.

There was very little light to illuminate the hall behind the man. But Danny was fearless, stepping over the drunk and shielding Junior as he led the way. Another person lay on the hallway floor, out cold, and something small scurried away before I could tell exactly what it was. Up a flight of stairs we went, finally reaching the cramped apartment where Junior lived. He introduced us to his mother and to children of various ages. They were just sitting down to dinner. A dinner of tuna fish—tuna-fish cat food, served directly from the can and spread on slices of bread. I wanted to cry. No wonder Junior had thought ours was the best tuna sandwich he'd ever tasted.

We didn't linger. We had just wanted to see that Junior made it home okay. His mom thanked us, and we left. I can't speak for Danny, but I was shaken. We made our way back down the dimly lit stairwell and onto the street in silence. However worldly we thought we were, at our core we were comparatively privileged white kids from families who loved us and could afford to provide us with good food. I've never forgotten the squalor at the homes of those two boys.

For weeks afterward, the boys showed up at our studio around lunchtime whenever they could, sometimes even playing hooky from school. They expected sandwiches or deviled eggs, fists full of crayons or just permission to play safely in front of the carriage house, knowing that they had protectors watching over them. In all honesty, the kids drove us both crazy when all we wanted to do was concentrate. But it was also satisfying to know that we were playing a part in introducing two underprivileged children to the idea that there was something else out there in the world for them, besides what they'd grown to know.

Predictable as clockwork, Diana the Witch invited herself over not long after. Taking me aside with her own peculiar brand of devilment shining in her face, she said, "You know, people will talk if two grown homosexual men have little boys visiting them all of the time." My face flashed hot with anger at the implication. If there was ever a moment in my life when I wanted to bitch-slap someone right across the face, it was that very moment. She made us feel compelled to tell the boys that they couldn't come over anymore, which is something I still feel bad about to this day.

I lost track of Junior; he and his family moved away. But somehow Diana became Scotty's foster parent and raised him, at least until I moved away. As crazy as she was, she could offer three square meals and an education to be found nowhere else on this earth. Plus, she had the forbearance to keep him in school. Forgive me if I repeat myself, but people are in my observation neither all good nor all bad, but a surprising and variable blending of both.

Danny Allen, Conté crayon on newsprint, 1973.
Collection of WTW.

Over time, as more and more Victorian houses became occupied and restored, the Cornhill District was starting to become solidly gentrified. Historic walking tours even traveled the district in better weather. This meant that Dan and I were in a constant state of negotiation with our landlady, Sally Rial, to keep her from raising our rent. We were just making do. For a while, we succeeded.

Mrs. Rial was an attractive woman of a certain age who carried herself as if she thought she was high society. Dan didn't like her, which was rare; Dan liked almost everyone. So I was left to ride our bicycle over to the more "fashionable" end of town to drop off the monthly rent check. I'd do my best to charm Mrs. Rial, playing Rachmaninoff's "Prelude in C Sharp Minor" for her on her polished baby grand piano, or sitting and having tea while complimenting her on her new hat or hairstyle. This is also known as Eddy Haskelling her, for anyone old enough to recognize the reference.

She owned several rental properties in Cornhill. Given the rising property values, she was more than making up for her ghetto investments by selling them off one at a time. One day when I presented her with our monthly check, she told me she was "considering" putting our home, along with the carriage house we loved, up for sale. "The market is right," she said. The news sent a cold wind through me.

Dan was less concerned, even when we got a note slipped under the side kitchen door telling us to expect a For Sale sign to go up within the next month or so. We continued our lives as if nothing was ever going to change. The prospect of losing our home was too difficult to face—not just the thought of moving all of our stuff, but the thought of having to leave a place we loved, a place that was so perfectly suited to our needs. We were living day to day, in a state of denial.

One afternoon, a month or two after we'd gotten that notice under the door, Dan told me he'd met some dude who was going to stop by and sell him an ounce of pot. I knew we couldn't afford it, but Danny wanted it all the same. However, when the guy arrived, Dan was outraged that what was being called a nickel bag was suddenly twenty-five freakin' bucks. I spoke up, offering to trade him a picture I'd done a year or two earlier. It was a vaguely psychedelic, art nouveau-style portrait I'd done of Eva Weiss, in pastel on board. I'd enhanced the portrait by gluing rhinestone junk jewelry all over the piece, leaving only Eva's face and hair showing. That dude must have been the dumbest dope dealer in the world because, stoned as he was, he offered us not one but two bags of pot for the picture—one of which Danny sold to the upstairs neighbors for thirty-five bucks, scoring us a tidy little profit.

We celebrated our spectacular score that night by setting out a supper of linguini in clam sauce and a bottle of cheap white wine. With the table set and the wine poured, we passed a joint back and forth, French-kissing and blowing the smoke in and out of each other's mouths while our candlelit dinner got cold.

There's no G-rated way of putting this: Danny pulled my chair away from the table, undid my jeans, and asked me to sit down. Kneeling in front of me, he was twirling linguini (ahem) around me repeatedly in a very arousing way and slurping the pasta into his mouth—when suddenly our side kitchen door opened and the lights flicked on. There stood our dumbfounded landlady, Sally Rial, with her contractor in tow, both stunned by the scene unfolding before them. Danny, swallowing a mouthful of pasta, looked her square in the eye and said, "It's the only way he can get me to eat." They both backed out of the kitchen in a quick-fast hurry.

It was abundantly clear; the deadline for our departure from the magic apartment with its perfect little carriage house was inevitable. We were going to have to find a new place to live, and fast.

Danny Allen, shadowbox assemblage, ca. 1970,
last known to be part of the estate of the late
Ramon Martinez. Whereabouts unknown.

THE CARRIAGE HOUSE was about to become history. Everything had to be boxed up for the move. Like it or not, Dan and I were faced with reluctantly leaving a place that still remains perfect in my memory. Change can be good or rough to confront, but it's a page that's always turning. It's inevitable— as inevitable as our efforts to resist it when it comes our way uninvited.

There's a myth about artists; people think we're all transients. That's hardly the case. Once an artist has a functioning, comfortable studio space where creativity flows freely, a proprietary sense grows that transcends leases and deeds. Not, however, in the eyes of the law. Were it up to me, I'd still be living in the apartment on Greenwood Street, making art in the carriage house with Dan. Dream as I may, that could never have come to pass. Change has a mind of its own, and we're all forced to follow its lead.

Even as we were supposed to be packing to move, Dan was spending his time writing or drawing and painting. I took the role of the practical one in our relationship, which isn't saying much for our combined grasp of reality.

While I packed and fretted, Dan often wrote and drew in notebooks. Even when I had good eyesight, it took an awful lot for me to be able to decipher his handwriting. His handwriting was beautiful, but it was so stylized that it was nearly impossible to read. Now, reading it is an even more daunting task, with my bilateral detached retinas on top of aging eyesight.

A page from one of Danny Allen's notebooks, photocopy. Date and whereabouts unknown.

I only have a partial set of Dan's writings—and all are photocopied pages given to me with great kindness by Eva Weiss.

Before Eva shared these writings with me, I had only read Dan's work on a couple of occasions. They were his personal material, and I never snooped. I read his poems years after he died, when Eva gave me the copies of the incomplete journal she had saved.

She gave me those copies on one of my rare return trips to Rochester. Two or more decades after Dan died, I attended a unique gathering there called the Gallucci Family Reunion. Supposedly there was an upstate New York crime syndicate known as the Gallucci Family. So we were the imposters—Dan's friends, and me by association. A bunch of crazies, we loosely referred to our group of creative ne'er-do-wells as the Gallucci Family. It was an inside joke that was probably a lot funnier at the time, with a joint in hand.

I went to the reunion with a subsequent boyfriend who'd barely been born by the time Dan died. That relationship was a part of an embarrassing midlife crisis. In any event, Eva gave me the copies of Dan's writings at the reunion, which was held in the garden of a Gothic Revival Victorian mansion that was available for special occasions. Lovely place, really, but in need of a little work, which made it the perfect setting for our gaggle of aging hippies.

As I held the pages close, I saw Diana snarl at me, casting shade my way. She said, "I know who you are, and you know I know who you are." Having never doubted Diana's words before, I took them at face value. I knew the same about her. But she was no doubt conjuring some sort of a devil's spell in my direction.

After Eva gave me the writings, an almost impossible chain of coincidences ensued, decades after Dan had left this life. On the train ride home to Philadelphia, I found myself stuck behind a derailed boxcar that took hours to set right. I don't usually like to read on the train, but pages from the past were sitting right on my lap, and the train wasn't going anywhere soon. What I had been given was an incomplete journal of Dan's day-to-day thoughts. He wrote a lot of jabberwocky in the style of avante-garde poets who had a following back in the day. It's difficult to read and decipher even when neatly written, but with

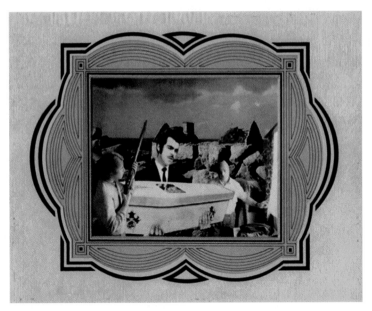

Danny Allen, THE GALLUCCI FAMILY WEDDING,
paper collage with rapidograph line-work, ca. 1970. Collection of WTW.

time on my hands and the determination to crack the code, I did read Dan's words—in his fascinating handwriting. The day was my birthday, July 29th, and I opened at random to an entry about me that was dated July 29, 1972.

Dan had been analyzing my personality based on astrological determinations from a book of astrology, which he'd probably borrowed from Diana's personal library. He was trying to understand the dynamic of the two of us together through the use of the stars. I've never put much stock in that sort of thing, but I thought it odd that I should be sitting on a train two decades after Dan was gone, reading his naïve but curiously accurate analysis of us based on the constellations. Then I found the following passage that still astonishes me:

> *It is a loving day today. Visitations and annunciations, plague me
> in skin; touching the most intimate part of my body, namely my
> brain. On a wooden train. Bill made love to me, I made love to Bill.
> Together we found the invisible line between people and banished it.*

In spite of the years that had passed, I felt an indescribable sensation of joy, remembering how it felt to be loved and to love my lover in return. It's not that

I'd forgotten those feelings, but rather that I'd consciously chosen not to dwell on what was gone forever. There I was in my forties, looking at photographs of Dan and reading his words through my middle-aged eyes. I had never before thought about him as merely an immature young person, a child who could grow a beard. He looked like an elfish young man with his whole life ahead of him. I reflected on how Pan-like Danny had been, on how he'd exuded both a gentleness of spirit and an aura of sensuality. Certain flavors, aromas, and music often triggered my memories of these qualities of his. Looking at the photos, I also remembered that Dan had been a really good cook when he put his mind to it—an intuitive cook, but a good one. I reflected on all the dinners he'd prepared me that had gotten cold because we'd chosen to make love instead. I couldn't understand why he'd snuffed out his young life by his own hand. I felt a parental longing as I looked back at the musings of a lost child who could never be recovered to safety.

Dan had died at 28, the same age as the man I was dating while in my forties, and I was exasperated by my new boyfriend's immaturity, glad that he'd driven home to Philadelphia before me. It turned out that he'd returned earlier to help orchestrate a surprise birthday party for me. When I finally arrived on my street, I was stunned to discover that I was hours late for my own party, which was well under way. My Philadelphia home is on a two hundred-year-old alley not open to cross traffic, making it perfect for street parties. As the guest of honor, I was arriving well after friends and neighbors were half drunk, their bellies full. Even before I could put down my bags, there were cards and gifts to open from friends.

After I'd opened them all, a neighbor said, "I almost forgot. A UPS package came for you earlier today." She went into her house to retrieve the package.

I must have had a startled expression on my face when I opened the box. It contained one of my favorite drawings of Dan's, and no note, only a return address. It was a picture titled *The Egyptian*, which he'd done in India ink on newsprint in 1973. I had always regretted parting with that particular drawing.

I later discovered that the note wasn't in the box because the sender, Phillip Byrd, had left a message on my 1990s desktop answering machine. I'd been friendly with Phillip toward the end of my stay in Rochester. His message told me that he was dying of AIDS and that his partner, Victor, who'd been a good friend of Dan's, had already passed away. Victor had asked Phillip, as their lives ebbed, to see to it that the drawing be sent back to me somehow. So Phillip made a search and found me, never knowing I was actually visiting Rochester as he was going through the enormous effort of sending that package down to Philadelphia.

Danny Allen, THE EGYPTIAN, India ink on newsprint, 1973. Collection of WTW.

Phillip was both moving and gracious in his message, telling me that he was resigned to his fate. I called him back right away. He wished me well and told me that Dan's art had gone through a series of owners, finding its way back home to me two decades later, on my 44th birthday—the very same day when I'd read Dan's journal and seen my astrological description in his own hand.

I treasure that drawing. It hangs over the headboard of my bed. The art has since born witness to my subsequent loves—or shall I say adventures? I never exactly fell in love again. I had crushes and attractions and short-lived affairs, even lived with a partner, but no one was Danny. He was the only one to whom I'd apply the word soulmate, in spite of our troubles. I wonder if Dan had any idea how much he was loved, not just by me, but by everyone.

Recently, Eva came down to visit me in Philadelphia and helped me decipher an epic poem Danny had written titled "Golden Nails on Blue Background." We had a glorious weekend, delving into the past and picking each other's brains for whatever might be left and still neurofiring. Eva remembers Danny taking her for a wheelbarrow ride that came to its conclusion only when they'd upended themselves into a bed of flowers, after which they'd no doubt placed the broken blossoms in their hair.

I should have seen through Dan's often-happy demeanor and realized that he was truly suffering. But I can be so observant and completely dense at the same time. I was too inexperienced to distinguish his genuinely troubled soul from the neurotic performances I'd seen in other eccentric creative types. I can recall Dan lighting one Marlboro off of another, smiling and looking at me like an inside joke was going through his mind, but there'd be no way for me to understand the travels of his thoughts, even if I asked him. He always looked so calm and wise. On closer inspection, I'd notice that his fingernails were gnawed down to the quick, barely leaving the white half-moons unbloodied. But he appeared so unphased.

I now understand that the Valium and the Quaaludes (called soapers on the street) were what made him that way. I never much cared for Quaaludes—nor for uppers or downers. I seem to have the opposite chemical reaction to those drugs than what they're supposed to produce. I tried them all, but ingestible highs aren't my thing. Dan kept his stash to himself, sharing only marijuana and hashish, knowing full well that both of those things made me horny. Whatever else was in his personal medicine cabinet was none of my concern, I thought. Foolishly, I chose not to look.

The drugs took us on some memorable journeys. I remember going to an art opening at the Memorial Art Gallery with Dan and a tiny, pretty young woman named Bernadette. Bernadette was petite and curvy, and she not only dressed like a gypsy but had the features to go along with the look. She could easily have passed for a Carmen or an Esmeralda. The name Bernadette seemed a bit too saintly for her, but it was just exotic enough that it fit. I have every reason to suspect that Bernadette, or more likely her biker boyfriend, was Danny's source for weed and hallucinogens.

Bernadette's boyfriend was a longhaired Viet Nam vet, heavily tattooed, which was uncommon back then. He had a habit of getting hammered on something or other and then of manhandling her. She'd sneak out to visit Dan while he was drawing or painting and visit with me by default. The boyfriend was more than a little rough around the edges; he was scary, always kicking Bernadette's two cats, Cannabis and Sativa. According to her, he called them Can 'o Piss and Saliva. Sometimes Bernadette had a black eye. Fortunately she didn't have one the evening we were escorting her to the art opening, but we were entrusted with hiding her from the boyfriend whose name, quite rightfully, I've forgotten.

We took her to the opening because the thug she lived with didn't even know where the art museum was, or that we had an art museum in the first place, so it would never have occurred to him to look for her there. Before leaving to take refuge with Dan and me, Bernadette had slipped a Quaalude into her erratic lover's beer while he was on the toilet. Our mission was to keep her hidden until he passed out, because he wouldn't recall anything in the morning. By noon he'd be sockin' her the good stuff the way she liked it, and when they were done, she'd cook him something to eat, and eventually their personal lifestyle pattern would start all over again, once he started to get drunk, high, or both.

Not always leaning toward good judgment, I had allowed Dan and Bernadette to talk me into trying a Quaalude for the first time. They'd already taken theirs. The fact that we were high on that particular drug had a lot to do with the slapstick events that unfolded.

For me, all art openings are alike. They're exhilarating for the artist in either a good or a bad way, but they're almost always a trial for me. Gallery openings have their own special lingo, bracketed between receiving air kisses and dodging people you don't want to get pinned against the wall listening to. Dan spoke the language of avante-garde art so I didn't have to. But for our exotic, dark beauty, Bernadette, this art opening was akin to Liza Doolittle's premier at Ascot. That said, the evening would not turn out so well for her.

The first thing one does at an art opening is figure out who the artist is, in case you should feel compelled to say something snarky about the work. Once said artist is located, everyone makes fake and fabulous compliments and then introduces the artist to anyone less savvy, so everyone else will be spared from hearing the artist's life story.

This particular opening was all fiber art—weavings mostly of the heavy, dark wool variety, with none-too-subtle undertones of giant pink vaginas hiding beneath the shaggy, oversized clumps of wool. Bernadette loved the works. So did Dan. I hadn't made my mind up about them when my Quaalude kicked in, and suddenly the work became more colorful and inspired, at the same time appearing obscenely comical and a tiny bit threatening. Several pieces bore wool tentacles that looked like they could self-propel away from the wall to suck in and swallow people whole. I couldn't stop laughing at the vision of someone being fed to the vaginal sculptures hung seductively on the walls, because everything experienced on Quaaludes seems hilarious. The whole world became my own private joke. But the drug didn't mellow me out; I felt like I could have run the fifty-yard dash.

Meanwhile, Dan and Bernadette seemed to be experiencing everything in slow motion. So why not get a clear plastic cup or two of cheap white wine and peruse the hors d'oeuvres table? There was a wide range to choose from, including little blocks of cheese in various shades of yellow and orange, as well as colorful red and green vegetables. I could tell from how brightly colored the food appeared that I was high, and my sense of equilibrium was compromised. All the same, I couldn't help but register dismay when I realized that Bernadette's peasant dress was largely constructed of patches of fabric that concealed hidden pockets throughout, and that she was gleefully filling each and every one of those pockets with fists full of cheese, pretzels, peanuts, and potato chips, with the intention of taking them home to feed her man.

Instinctively I moved away from her, as if I'd never seen her before in my life. Danny was practically collapsed in a corner, laughing, while Bernadette did her grocery shopping. She was very good at it. In fact, people standing right next to her seemed not to notice a thing. She discovered radishes, celery, and sliced cucumbers next to a bowl of dip and made off with many of them, accomplishing her entire heist while encumbered with dozens of gypsy bracelets. What she failed to take into account was the unsteadiness that can accompany a Quaalude high and the short flight of stairs nearby. She spun on her heels, lost her footing, and tumbled down the stairs. Her bracelets caught hold of her complicated skirt as she threw her hands in the air, attempting to right herself, thus launching fistfuls of bridge mix into the stair hall. Inadvertently, Bernadette pelted a nineteenth-century French Academic painting by William Adolf Beaugureau with peanuts, popcorn, and cheese squares, which became lodged between the image of a winged angel and its antique Barbizon picture frame. The gentlemen who failed in their efforts to catch Bernadette were rewarded for their attempted gallantry by the fact that Bernadette made a practice of never wearing underwear.

Danny and I knew we had to stop laughing and hustle her the devil out of there. We collected her from off the landing and left to sober ourselves up on coffee at an all-night diner.

Years later, I received a letter from the State of California Board of Corrections asking about Bernadette's character. They wanted me to give them some reasons why they should parole her after a conviction for drug possession. She was a sweet kid, and I told them that life owed her a break. There was a questionnaire attached, and one of the questions was, "What sort of career training might best suit this individual?" Not finding anything on the list that brought her skill set to mind, I checked "other." Using the space provided on the line below, I wrote "food services and catering."

But I've allowed myself to wander off track yet again, so before derailing myself once more, I'd best get around to describing how Danny and I were moving from Cornhill to Merriman Street, not entirely of our choosing.

Bill Whiting, ca. 1973.
Stockbroker's Tudor.
This East-Avenue-style
Tudor dollhouse bears
resemblance to our home
on Merriman Street.
Collection of the Toy
and Miniature Museum
of Kansas City.

It's the physical act of moving that vexes me the most. I hate packing things and dragging shit from pillar to post. Granted, most of the junk was mine for this particular move, but a little help would have been nice. Dan mostly laughed at my lack of progress, knowing it would all eventually get done. Pizza and beer always seem to do the trick in getting other people motivated to help during a move—and the same cheap bribe can get your apartment painted, as well.

I don't recall how we found our new apartment on Merriman Street, between East and University Avenues. I think a friend told us about it. The address was 105 Merriman, if memory serves me. We lugged tons of things over on foot. Sometimes one of us rode ahead on our fat-tired bicycle. Then we'd make the trek up four flights of stairs to our new attic apartment in a once-magnificent Queen Anne Victorian. Our new apartment was the entire top floor, with dormer windows, turrets, and towers. We were moving into one of the rattier buildings that was still affordable in the fashionable East Avenue section of town, on the other side of the Genesee River from Cornhill. We could walk to our old neighborhood, but it was enough of a hike that we felt like we were miles away—especially while lugging boxes of books and records.

The first thing we learned about Merriman Street was the necessity for well-placed buckets in strategic locations during rainstorms. Roofs full of turrets and dormers are always quick to leak. Come winter, we even experienced indoor snowdrifts through the drafty, century-old windows. The radiators tended to be lukewarm, except for the one in the middle room, on which you could fry an egg.

Dan's friend David Lortz moved most of our large things in his classic Volkswagen hippie bus. We loaded it with furniture and hauled everything across town to our new home—all except for one item that required a pick-up truck. During our last days on Greenwood Street, Dan had found a fancy, golden-oak, upright piano in an abandoned house in south Cornhill. He'd had it tuned as a gift for me. It looked like it belonged in the saloon in an old Western movie. I loved it.

Confessions are in order: Dan and I both stand guilty as charged. We entered abandoned Victorian houses in Cornhill and made off with some very cool stuff. Sometimes we ran into other looters and negotiated with a wink and a nod what items which vandal was going to take. Later in life, as a staunch believer in historic preservation, I find that my only defense is to swear that we saved far more things than we spoiled. However, I still think about an ancient, square grand piano from which Dan and I took the fancy-scrollwork music stand and bench—only to return to find that someone else had taken the piano right out from under us. If I'd known who'd taken it, I'd have given them what we had. It all belonged together. Oh, well. Square grands never hold a tune, anyway.

Photo by Dan Allen. Dan and Eva (bellbottomed leg) in a mirror in a house in Cornhill, ca. 1970.

That piano escaped us, but Dan was still determined to get me a piano, in spite of the hard truth that my musical compositions should never really have been encouraged. I'd compose unlistenable music while Dan worked at his drafting table, but my playing didn't appear to bother him. Maybe love is not only blind, but also tone deaf. I wasn't all that bad, really—but my piano skills were at best sophomoric. I wouldn't have stood a chance next to a student from Rochester's prestigious Eastman School of Music.

Friends, along with some very strong University of Rochester frat boys, helped us get that mother-fucking piano up four flights of stairs on an unseasonably hot and humid day. I think it was one of those rogue warm days in fall that feels like summer, only to be followed by a cold snap. I know it was well before Danny and I had learned about our indoor snowdrifts.

Ostensibly we had the whole floor to ourselves, but in fact we shared the apartment with mysterious roommates who could be heard but never seen. They couldn't see us, either—or anything else, for that matter. Our bedroom was an octagonal bay tower overlooking the street, directly next to a decorative rooftop spire for which there was no interior access. But we could hear rustlings inside that space. I didn't want to know what was going on in there, but our cats, Natasha Sweetmeat and Jalapeño Pushpin the Ping-Pong Pal, were fascinated. Their eyes would follow unseen movement and sounds from behind the wall. It freaked me out.

While I was reminiscing recently with Susan Plunkett, one of Rochester's best cooks ever, she told me, "The last time I saw Danny was at night on Park Avenue in Rochester, and the sky was full of schools of bats. I never forgot that." I asked her if she knew where those bats had come from—because I did. They'd come from inside that sealed-off tower in the house on Merriman Street. The fates had seen fit to place two bat-shit crazy, artistic fruits on one side of the wall and hundreds of fruit bats on the other.

Although Natasha and The Pushpin were indoor cats, when we'd leave the windows open for whatever reason, they would explore the roof and even get themselves into the tree limbs hanging over the eaves. I didn't blame them. For a cold-weather city, Rochester could have some sweltering hot days in season. Our multifaceted, diamond-cut rooflines all joined together, so the sun was always cooking the treeless side of our apartment on warm days. You could go from broiling to freezing merely by moving from one room to the next.

One night, Dan and I were making dinner in the kitchen when a warm rain starting coming down sideways. I turned to close the kitchen dormer window just as Natasha jumped from another part of the roofline toward the window. It was one of those awful moments when things seem to happen in slow motion, yet all at once and in the blink of an eye. I was horrified as I struggled to get the window back open, watching Natasha hover in thin air and desperately paw at the windowpane like some Warner Brothers' cartoon character. The poor thing wound up falling four stories into a basement window well full of leaves. Dan and I ran down the stairs to the outside of the house just in time to see Natasha pop her head up, wearing a maple leaf that was stylishly stuck to the top of her head. Dan picked her up and assessed that she had no injuries. He held her so her sticky maple-leaf hat was shown from the best angle and lovingly said so that I could hear, "Tomorrow you shall wear a full face of make-up." All was well except for the spaghetti boiling over on the stovetop.

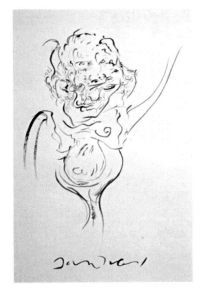

Danny Allen, ink drawing of multiple bat-like faces, ca. 1970. Collection of WTW.

Another warm summer evening, when the roof was retaining the heat of the day, we opened all the windows and lay in bed to rest. Natasha Sweetmeat sat on the ledge of the windowsill, watching the bats fly past. Suddenly she reached out with one claw and pulled a bat into the house. She jumped onto the bed to show me her trophy while the bat's wings flapped all over my bare chest. I screamed like a woman, and Danny got the poor flying beast away from her. The bat was so badly injured that Danny had to put it out of its misery—so he clocked it with a miter box. Unbeknownst to me, he then put the remains in a jar that used to hold marinated artichoke hearts and refrigerated the animal so he could study it at a later date.

Come the next day, at around noon, I went scrounging for some lunch. Loving marinated artichoke hearts, I opened the jar and was so grossed-out I nearly screamed all over again. Have you ever seen a bat's face up close? It looks like a split-open walnut shell with features that barely resemble a face. Dan doubled over with laughter until he could barely breathe. I've never eaten marinated artichoke hearts since. I can't even walk past the jars in the supermarket.

The bat incidents became a regular occurrence, and eventually I stopped freaking out about them. But I'll never forget one night when Adele Fico was over and a bat got into the apartment, making that horrible noise they make. Bats let out an otherworldly, seemingly electronic sound when captured or injured. Adele locked herself in the bathroom, screaming at the top of her lungs while standing on the toilet seat, holding a towel over her head. As if bats were really going to make a nest in her hair. Dan used the miter box once again that night, and later he wore that same bat on a string hung around his neck as a part of a Halloween costume.

Bats are wonderful and useful animals, but their presence in the Merriman Street apartment dramatically curbed my appetite. They made me squeamish. I admit that it disgusted me to live in a place where bats were constantly getting in the house. But Dan became somewhat of an expert on bats. His friend Greg, who is a straight guy, once called Dan to come over and remove a bat from his apartment. Stereotypes would make a person think the gay guy would be the one who was squeamish about bats (like me). But this was not the first time Dan had come to Greg's rescue.

Greg and Danny had been roommates in San Francisco, where they lived with a girl named Gayle, who supported them both during the mid-1960s. This was during the height of the Vietnam War, and Greg, with good reason, was scared to death of being drafted. When his draft notice arrived, Danny coached him on how to act like a gay guy convincingly. Dan then attested to Greg being his lover, hence awarding Greg 4-F status and quite possibly saving his life.

Greg told me recently that Danny had told him about his own time in the military, after he'd dropped out of college at the Fashion Institute of Technology and thus lost his student deferment. I was floored. This was the first time I'd heard anything about Dan having been in the service. Nearly forty years later, the man remains an enigma within a conundrum.

But back to the bats. When Dan got over to Greg's house to capture the bat hanging from the crown molding, the bat had already died. Danny's natural reaction was to pin the dead beast to the front of his T-shirt with its wings spread wide open and to wear it home as if it were a brooch.

Despite the bat problems, our new Merriman Street location had a great deal to recommend it. East Avenue was every bit as interesting and eccentric as the Cornhill District. We weren't far from the George Eastman House of Photography, where silent-screen legend Louise Brooks lived in comparative seclusion. She was a thin and frail woman who moved about in a labored way, burdened by the pains of aging. A Louise Brooks sighting in Rochester was akin to a Garbo sighting in New York.

Once we saw her in an unexpected location. Our neighborhood offered great trash, and Dan and I were inveterate trash pickers. I liked finding useful or beautiful things discarded by others, and Dan was always on the lookout for odd objects to incorporate into his Josef Cornell-style shadowboxes. While I was on the lookout for old chairs or lamps, Danny was captivated by parts of things, by bits and pieces that could be glued together as assemblage art.

One day, word reached us that a huge pile of things was sitting out in front of one of the mansions of East Avenue that had been doomed to demolition. Of course we had to go scope out the offerings. As we approached the site, a neighbor stopped us and told us to look but not to go any closer. And there she was, Louise Brooks, selecting something small and mysterious from the pile of junk. We watched in silence as a man urged her back toward the Eastman House of Photography, home not only to the star herself but also to so many of the classic photos that featured her in the prime of her beauty.

If a renowned movie star of the silent-screen era could pick something out of a trash pile, then that more than legitimized our doing the same. Earlier, the iconic Ms. Brooks had liberated women with her chic yet practical fashions and her sensuality. Now, she gave our rummaging through the trash an aura of legitimacy that it hadn't possessed before. As if anything would have stopped us.

Louise Brooks was not the only dignified relic from the silent-screen era who lived nearby. Hildegard and James Sibley Watson weren't far away. He was the heir to the fortune his family earned as founding owners of the Western Union Company, not to mention the Sibley, Lindsay & Curr department-store chain. The Watsons lived on none other than Sibley Place, right off East Avenue. In 1933,

James had produced an experimental silent film titled *Lot in Sodom*—starring his wife, Hildegard, as Lot's wife, who's turned into a pillar of salt. It's one of those silent biblical epics. One can watch the films of Louise Brooks and the Watsons on YouTube to get a real sense of who lived in the neighborhood.

The Watsons always had season tickets to everything but never went. They were very sweet and referred to us as "those two nice young men." One of them would call us on the phone to let us know they had tickets for us to the Eastman Theater, and when I'd go to their house, most of the time a servant would come to the door and hand me the tickets. But sometimes I'd enter their home, with its grand sweeping staircase. Things were a bit cluttered, with piles of ironing and other items lying about. In addition to the house, they had an outbuilding that was decorated inside with a set from a silent film, which they probably left in place as a reminder of the energizing projects that come with being young.

These seemingly unusual characters and locations were typical of Rochester. Nothing you could ever tell me about that town would surprise me. People there prided themselves on their peculiarities, some of which were unusual to the extreme. The most classic eccentric old lady in the neighborhood was Charlotte Whitney Allen. Charlotte (no relation to Danny) lived in a magnificent house on Oliver Street. She had a stunning garden designed by Fletcher Steele, with a robust Gaston Lachaise sculpture dominating her urban landscape. Artists get to be everyone's poor relative when it comes to party invitations, so all the artists and attractive gay men in Rochester eventually received an invitation to attend one of Charlotte Allan's daily martini parties at 5:30 p.m. sharp, and you'd better look snappy.

Charlotte's favorite color was black. She wore black hats, black dresses, black shoes, and black stockings, all while riding around in her black limousine driven by her black chauffeur. While she was a patron of the musical arts, she despised the human voice when lifted in song. She loved music, mind you; she merely hated hearing people sing. I recall sitting in the Eastman Theater with Dan and our friend Josef, with Charlotte Allen seated on the aisle a row or two in front of us. The grand old gal was settling in for a lovely evening of Mozart or Beethoven when she opened her program to discover that she was attending a hundred-voice performance of Carl Orff's *Carmina Burana*. She started to pitch a fit for help. Getting out of her seat with full silent-movie-actress drama, she feigned distress. Her chauffeur ran up from the back of the theater, administered her smelling salts, and aided her spindly little body toward the exit, presumably to the limousine. All the while, a huge cast of vocalists sang out at the top of their lungs. Danny, Josef, and I could not so much as look at each other during the remainder of the performance without going into peals of laughter, disturbing everyone around us.

There existed, in the Rochester of my recollection, a kind of salon society. I don't know if it was the era or Rochester's severe winters that caused this, but we were positioned to experience hospitality from eccentric people across the spectrum, from hippie to chic and all variations in between, and we were lucky to have generous people in our lives. Winters were always long and brutal, so Rochesterians held brunches and dinner parties in their homes. Some were hippie parties, with giant bowls of pasta and salad and the Grateful Dead playing in the background on albums while a bong was passed around the room. Others were sophisticated experiments in nostalgia and polite culture, reintroducing quiche Lorraine and upscale versions of peasant cuisine like cassoulet, washed back with Mimosas or Bloody Marys. We balanced our eclectic friendships, moving between elegant society and our own hippie, granola-muffin poverty. Through it all, Dan and I had each other, until we did not.

Because of their precipitous end, my roughly three years with Danny remain an unresolved chapter in my life. I'm not a big believer in the existence of closure—it seems to me like a mysterious and unachievable goal that people attempt to reach but never entirely succeed at obtaining. The best any of us can hope for is to make a benign pact with loss and do our best to live, sometimes withdrawing into our tender and raw remembrances.

Dan mesmerized me, as he did so many other people. Part of the draw was his pure creative energy and his mysterious worldview that challenged everything you thought you knew. He had the aura of a sprite or a fawn. Not just now in hindsight, but even back then, when he was flesh and blood before my very eyes, Danny seemed mythological. Had he started to play the panpipes and grown goat hooves and a prehensile tail, it wouldn't have surprised me in the least. Then again, we did take drugs.

I like to remember Danny looking up from a drawing or painting he was working on, holding a cigarette, and laughing in his bright and boyish way. I'll save his darker side for later. For now, I'll remember Dan as light and laughter, silliness and fun—a man with his own peculiar outlook that helped shape my own.

Dan was not only my lover but also my art instructor, even though it was I who smuggled him into art lectures and workshops while I was a paying art student. I learned more about art from him than I did from any paid professor. Dan possessed a natural gift for expressing his imagination through his art, as if being self-taught had kept his creativity pure. I am by comparison a literal interpreter of what I see. I'm a kind of human visual-recording device. Dan could see past the exterior and into the soul—and express it—even if what he expressed was troubling.

Now that I'm older, people turn to me assuming I've got wisdom that I'm not sure I possess—though I do know what roads not to travel. If I have any wisdom at all, it's been hard won, earned more through experience than by listening to or applying anyone else's advice. But Dan always knew things.

Not long after Dan and I moved to the Merriman Street apartment, Dan asked me in a very matter-of-fact way, "If I commit suicide, would you follow me?" Stunned, I said, "Hell, no!" I thought he was looking for sympathy or being melodramatic. But he appeared visibly hurt by my reply and withdrew into his private thoughts. Were someone to ask me that same question today, nearly forty years later, I'd fly into action, doing whatever I could to guide that person to safety. Yet hardly anyone knows anything useful in his or her early twenties. I certainly didn't.

Danny Allen, India ink,
ca. 1974.
Collection of WTW.

Danny Allen, The Visitor, *acrylic on board, 18 x 24 inches, ca 1973.*
Collection of Eva Weiss.

At some point, this question must be addressed: What is *crazy*? People use the word too loosely and without any genuine understanding. Is it madness? Insanity? All of those words are tainted with prejudice. Humans have a tendency to allow the troubling components of someone else's personality to outweigh all the good that dwells within that person's soul. Bad seems to weigh more than good, dark more than light. Whether in darkness or in light, Dan was far more fragile than anyone around him guessed he was.

Was Dan crazy, or was it the drugs that drove him over the edge? It's up for debate how much of a role drugs played in Dan's life choices and in his decision to take his own life. Back then, among the people we knew, drugs were viewed as neither good nor bad. We were naïve to the extreme. We were the experimental generation.

Looking at Dan's face and its structure, I often wondered if he had any Native American blood in his heritage. Having studied portraiture and occasionally earned my living at it, I've come to know faces, and there were angles to Danny's face that bring Native American facial structure to mind and that lent him a quality of nobility. In reading and transcribing what little remains available of his writings, I think that Dan was a cultural borrower, at the least. He had his own belief system, with elements from Eastern philosophy and the remnants of a Catholic upbringing. But there was something more in Dan's words, indicating that he believed a better life waited for him after this world of flesh was over. That much is Catholic. But he seems to have believed that he could get there on his own. Influenced by various sources, with a fertile mind almost too intelligent for his own good, Danny may have believed that he could make that leap (and I don't use the word lightly) toward life after death.

Yet beliefs weren't the whole story. Never underestimate the impact of recreational drugs and how those drugs can be at odds with prescription medications, as well as body chemistry and other predispositions. I believe that all of these factors played a part in what formed Dan's thinking during the last difficult years of his life.

Danny Allen, India ink, 1972.
Collection of WTW.

In Dan's own words,

Maturing is like frying, as damp is to drying on a doorway to death. It is closer with each word that I write and you read. Ticking. The time is fleshing away used cells, replacing them with ones which may be stronger but not last longer

This sense of becoming decrepit as he aged was probably another factor in Dan's mental suffering. Dan was a gay youth who had been viewed as beautiful. I say *had* because his self-image was becoming dysmorphic even before I'd met him. Dan had physically aged early, at least in his mind's eye. He had gone from a beautiful flower child to a prematurely balding young man. And hippies defined their defiance by sporting long hair, so hippie dudes who were losing their hair felt self-conscious and left out. Here we were, rebelling against established norms by altering our appearances in protest, only to become victims of style, not agents of social change.

Dan shocked everyone when he shaved his head smooth, back when hardly anyone did that. His features were so aristocratic that in many ways a bald head made him handsomer—but that look had not yet come into style, so it shocked the very people who considered themselves to be shocking. Friends and associates were startled, though few would give a thing like a shaved head a second thought today.

To some, his impulsive action may have seemed erratic. But I knew at least some of what lay behind it. Dan was fascinated by a couple named Jim and Roxanne. Roxanne was a pre-Raphaelite beauty, with wavy blond hair and a lean, willowy figure. Her boyfriend, Jim, was an Adonis, with long, raven-black hair. They were a physically stunning couple and would have been no matter what the styles had been during any era. They were nice enough as people, but their magnetism came from what was skin deep. Dan knew better than to denigrate himself for having thinning hair, but everyone feels the ache of wanting to belong to Jim and Roxanne's share of the world.

So Dan chose to set himself apart from everyone by shaving his head bald. He dared to rebel against the rebels. But in his insecurity about changing from a pretty flower child to a balding man, Dan felt an inner loathing for his imperfections, for not being Jim or Roxanne. It's no different than what millions of

Danny Allen working on a psychedelic ceiling mural, ca. 1968.
Location and survival unknown.

people feel daily when confronted with impossibly perfect models in Ralph Lauren ads. This is a futile waste of time, but it's also human nature (not to mention a powerful way to get people to buy products they don't need). Dan was now the bald dude who did a few more drugs than everyone else. But more than his hairstyle was changing; I believe this was when he entered the secret world of bathhouses and had a heightened number of anonymous sexual encounters.

This was not a world for which I had a natural empathy. Neither was the world of serious drug users. Later in life, I came to have a better understanding of how destabilizing the combination of drugs and obsessive sexual behavior could be, especially for someone who is already troubled.

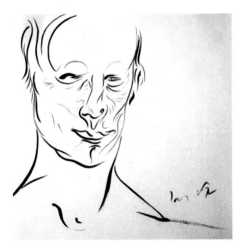

Danny Allen, India ink sketch, 1972.
Collection of WTW.

And I knew by then that Dan was troubled. He had always displayed moments of darkness, which counterbalanced his light, almost childlike optimism. The clouds would lift, and expressions of a better self would emerge, endearing me to him and erasing disturbing memories—at least for the moment. Life with Danny was a continual up-and-down, a series of rapid switches between polar-opposite frames of mind, often connected to whether he was sober or high.

I think most thoughtful artists embrace a range of emotions and draw from those feelings to express the full experience of life. They live with a box of crayons that contains more than just the bright and cheerful colors. But more often than most people, Dan got stuck in the darker, more troubling hues.

I didn't understand how serious this was. When the person you love is perched on the edge of a psychological disorder, you feel like you're in the eye of a storm. Dark clouds are all around you, but things seem fine from where you're standing. An enabling sense of denial allows you to continue on.

Not only that, but I was absorbed in my own problems, my own life, my own goals. It wasn't until Dan's emotional imbalance became so acute that there was no longer any ignoring it that I became frightened. Yet even when I was afraid of Dan, an act of gentleness from him would re-endear him to me, and I'd erase our conflicts from my thoughts. Sometimes we talked about breaking up. We lived in a state of on-again, off-again while remaining under the same roof, still making love. Sometimes we drifted apart, but there was never a time when I didn't love him.

All too frequent, however, were the times when I didn't understand him. It has been said to me—and reinforced by my own observations—that much of Dan's work resembles art done by mental patients. I'm no expert on the subject, but I recognize and understand the comparison.

Danny Allen, India ink study sketch of THE VISITOR. *1972.*
Collection of WTW.

The works pictured in this chapter are mostly sketch variations of a series he called *The Visitor.* He drew more versions of these odd and haunting faces than I have access to. He threw some of them away, but he kept returning to this fundamental image, sometimes with a foreshortened figure, always with troubled eyes. I have no idea where all of them have gone, nor do I know who or what they represent. Often the figures appear to be male, at other times female, but clearly they all depict the same character. Some versions are boldly drafted, while others are so faint that it's difficult to photograph them without digitally enhancing the lines. Some of the pieces are starting to fade, in spite of having been stored in the dark.

*Danny Allen, India ink sketch, 1972.
Collection of WTW.*

The Visitor drawings have always held an ominous and troubling association for me. I don't choose to look at them very often. Many evoke malevolence and confusion. How one interprets art is up to the viewer, however, and what this series meant to Dan is as mysterious to me now as it was when he was alive.

*Danny Allen, India ink sketch,
1972. Collection of WTW.*

Diana the Witch would frequently make comparisons between Danny and Vincent van Gogh. Dan didn't live long enough to acquire the body of accomplished work that van Gogh has to his credit, and I'm not suggesting any unfair comparisons between them. But bearing Diana's assertions in mind, I went to the Philadelphia Museum of Art in 2012 to see a retrospective of van Gogh's work. There are easy, obvious comparisons. Both were talented young men with a self-destructive streak, and both eventually committed suicide. Dan jumped off a bridge, and the story of van Gogh's death in 1890 suggests that he might have shot himself in the chest and took almost thirty hours to die, fully conscious, as doctors were unable to remove the bullet to save him.

Danny Allen, India ink sketch with an exaggerated example of movement lines, 1972. Collection of Eva Weiss.

I was viewing the van Gogh exhibit with a fellow painter, and I noted that everything in the paintings, from fruit and flowers to buildings and trees, gave off the appearance of being in the midst of an earthquake. I said to her, "Only van Gogh could paint a floral arrangement and make it look like a nervous wreck." I was being flippant. But the moment I said it, I realized that Dan's work also has those nervous, staccato movement-lines. It's as if there was never a sense of rest or peace for either of them. I hadn't taken in that similarity before because Dan created his nervous lines mostly in black ink on white paper, while Van Gogh used color. But there is the same sense of everything trembling with nervous energy.

Danny Allen, India ink on bond,
ca. 1970. Collection of WTW.

Not long after Dan and I had moved to Merriman Street, he was offered a job at the Rochester Memorial Art Gallery. The job involved him working as a janitor in the mornings and assisting the curatorial staff in the afternoons. At first I thought this would be a great opportunity for him. It seemed like the ideal way to study art and to get to participate in hanging exhibits. It would have been great for him to have access to the art-storage rooms, because he would get to study things not regularly on display.

But Danny couldn't handle the job emotionally. He found it demeaning, especially after being caught cleaning the men's room by an RIT student he knew, who was in the museum to hang his own one-man show. Dan cried at night, expressing a panic that his life as an artist was going to be devalued to that of a janitor cleaning toilets in a museum where other people's art was displayed. After a week or less on the job, he refused to go back.

Since Dan's museum job paid far more than my job at the department store, I phoned in to my own job and gave notice. I went in to the museum the very next day as if I were Dan. I literally picked up the mop and did the job. And as bizarre as it sounds, the museum's paperwork was changed, and I was hired. It's difficult to imagine an employee transfer happening that way in today's world.

Right away, I understood exactly how Dan had felt. It was demeaning to scrub toilets and mop bathroom floors. But I also mopped gallery floors in the company of a fine collection of art and artifacts, which allowed me to linger over pieces that most patrons merely glanced at in passing. I wish Dan could have toughed it out and stayed with the job long enough to enjoy its benefits.

I wish a lot of things. I wish I hadn't harped on him about practical issues like money. We were perpetually late with our rent and frequently had next to nothing in the refrigerator. I would become shrill, complaining about our inability to make ends meet, saying things I regretted, emphasizing that I was the one holding down a nine-to-five job while I rarely knew what Dan did with his days—and, sometimes, his nights. When Dan got paid for a freelance job, his priority was buying an ounce of pot or scoring other kinds of drugs.

If wishes came true, the museum job would have been as good for him as it was for me. My supervisors never treated Dan or me like we were subservient. In fact, we were frequently invited to their homes for dinner parties, where they introduced us to other artists, writers, and musicians. But full-time jobs didn't work for Danny. He didn't care to answer to anyone. Who does? Still, most of us accept that reality.

Nevertheless, I was willing to continue supporting Dan, despite all the nights when he didn't return home and the days when his activities were unaccounted for. One of my greatest shortcomings is fierce loyalty; I'll endure conduct in a relationship that most people would never stand for. As if knowing this, Dan strayed farther and farther away from normalcy.

I rescued a kitten from the street one day, on my way home from the art gallery. For its own safety, I kept the poor thing in a box behind a closed bathroom door, since the other cats clearly wanted to kill it. The kitten was sick and eventually died. Then Dan got me an orange kitten we named Lucille Ball to take the place of the one that hadn't made it.

Unfortunately, Lucille was full of more energy than any cat I'd ever seen. She was prone to destroying whatever was in her path. She clawed everything we owned, including one of my dollhouses, resulting in extensive repairs shortly before the piece was due to go on display.

With maturity comes clarity—clarity that neither Dan nor I was mature enough to possess. People cannot relate to an animal as if it were another person. But foolishly, I tried to. When I found the damaged dollhouse that I was preparing to show at the Memorial Art Gallery, I screamed at Lucille at the top of my lungs and spanked her with a rolled-up newspaper. That kind of corporal punishment makes no impression on a cat—in fact, that was the old-school method for training a dog, and no one in his or her right mind trains any animal that way today. And Danny was particularly sensitive to the mistreatment of animals. He had worked at an animal shelter called Lollipop Farms briefly and had been traumatized to see that the animals were euthanized nearly as fast as they arrived. He left after only a couple of weeks, but the scars on his psyche were wreaking havoc. Eva said, "Danny thought all he'd be doing was cleaning bunny cages, and he found himself disposing of the corpses of animals he'd grown to love."

So when I hit our kitten, Dan became furious with me. For some reason, this led him to drown the kitten in a bucket when I was out. I didn't know where he or the kitten had gone for two days or more, but finally he came back home, riddled with angst and shame. He collapsed on the floor, crying, wailing, and begging for forgiveness. I had a sick feeling in my heart and my gut when he told me he'd drowned Lucille. Between his tears he asked, "What's wrong with me?" I had no satisfactory answer to give him, because I honestly didn't know.

Soon after that, Dan started to see a psychotherapist. He was put on medication, an early, experimental version of what was later called Prozac. Unfortunately, that didn't prevent him from partying with Quaaludes (downers) and Black Beauties (uppers) or from drinking and smoking pot—or taking things of mysterious origin from people he didn't know all that well.

There's no possible way to describe what it's like to be in love with a person and to feel invested in your relationship while living in denial that your partner is losing his grasp on reality. I have no doubt that by this time in our relationship, Dan, for whatever reasons, popped in and out of sanity. Those days weren't anything like the times we'd spent in the carriage house on Greenwood Street, and even back then I'd missed all the warning signs.

My own denial about the kitten incident took on a weird kind of self-absorbed guilt. I kept telling myself that I hadn't done anything to actually harm Lucille, but I felt nevertheless as if I had drowned her, since I believed that my actions had driven Dan to extreme and disturbing measures. I couldn't tell that, while what I had done was unkind, what he had done was a red-flag warning of a sickness and that his action shouldn't be excused as a reaction to my mistake.

Another disturbing incident stemmed from a running argument I'd had with my former college roommate, Marc, who had taken a liking to a painting I'd done my senior year. The subject of the painting was a pair of male nude figures with swans emerging from the tops of their heads in a surreal setting. I think the painting would probably embarrass me if I saw it today, but back then it was very au courant. Marc offered to trade me an Empire settee for the painting. I agreed, gave Marc the painting, and never got the settee. Marc, who'd recently emerged from an ugly divorce, instead gave me one of his own huge canvases in trade. It depicted a violent interaction between a man and a woman, both nude, and it looked like a rape scene. I didn't like it and didn't want it in the house, not to mention that he hadn't kept our bargain.

Dan took on my anger and became incensed. One day while I was at work, Dan broke into Marc's apartment to take my painting back. The police were called, and the entire thing became a gigantic, entangled mess. Fortunately, charges were dropped, so it never went to court. Dan told me that he was trying to get the painting back to prove to me that he loved me. He felt ashamed and disappeared again, and I never got the settee. Frankly, it no longer mattered. Our relationship had lost all sense of normalcy, and I was in over my head.

After incidents like that, Dan and I lived in prolonged periods of silence. Perfunctory actions like dinner and laundry were cloaked in denial, all taking place without any real communication. I'm not sure whether I didn't know what to ask Dan concerning his frame of mind or whether I was afraid to ask. Given the way I'd been raised, it should have come as no surprise that I tried to wipe the bizarre incidents from my thoughts and to pretend they hadn't happened.

Dan took to not coming home at night or to getting in extremely late. I didn't know if he'd spent the time at a friend's place or a bathhouse, on the streets or with another lover or a trick. What was clear, when I allowed myself to think about it, was that our relationship was falling apart, and so was Dan.

Late one afternoon, Dan came home wild-eyed and agitated. He appeared to be on something, and his usually tranquil exterior had given way to a person not so different from the people he drew with quivering movement lines surrounding them. He forced me to sit in a chair in the middle of the room for what might have been fifteen minutes or three hours. He circled me while holding a kitchen knife, screaming at me and jabbing the knife in my direction if I so much as moved. Eventually, he dropped the knife and ran out, slamming the door behind him. Again he didn't come home for a while, and he cried and begged for forgiveness when he returned. It was that incident that spurred me to bring up the topic of our breaking up.

A mutual friend of Dan's and mine who now counsels university students offered me advice not long ago. He and I have often discussed Danny, as he'd known us as a couple and also separately as friends. He said, "Some people fall off the deep end. No one knows why. It just happens."

So what I'm left to tell doesn't offer much by way of closure. What happened happened. But those troubling experiences are not the sum total of Dan's life or his personality. His dark side was a part of him, and that's all. I'm at a loss to explain it, but I still love Dan, or, at the very least, my memory of him.

When Dan died, friends shipped me off to New York to spend two weeks with a mutual friend who'd recently moved there. Back then, a gay lover wasn't someone the world felt compelled to comfort or include in a church funeral. It wasn't Dan's family who made the decision to leave me out of the funeral, however. It was our friends, who perhaps meant well. They believed it would be best if I didn't attend the service.

I didn't ask questions; I did as I was told. I went to New York in a daze and stayed with a fellow named Frank. I don't have much recollection of that time away. I mostly remember wandering around and feeling lost, dropping money on the ground, not wanting to be there or to go home, not knowing what I wanted. When I came back to Rochester, friends had moved me to a new apartment on University Avenue. They were trying to help and protect me, and I greatly appreciate their intentions, but this might not have been the best thing for me. Without getting to see Dan buried, without having our apartment as a place where I could sift through my memories, I became suspended in an unresolved frame of mind that I'm only now discussing at length, almost forty years later.

I think about Danny every single day, while at the very same moment trying to put him out of my thoughts. I've had decades to confront my own demons, but they're still there, as omnipresent as ever. As Dan wrote in his journal,

> *Psycho-anal-yzed, psycho-anal eyezd, psycho-anal-eyesed. Psycho-anal-eyes. A penis stuck in an eye cavity. Or, a penis with an eye on its head looking into someone's asshole. Or, doctor you are an ass hole trying to fuck me.*

Clearly, Dan mistrusted the professionals who tried to help him. As for me, I was ill equipped to cope with the level of unrest eating away at the person I loved, transforming him into someone beyond recognition. I was transforming, too, into someone more distant and concerned with my own preservation. I had all but lost touch with the gentle young man I'd fallen in love with, the Danny I still prefer to remember.

Danny Allen, sketch of the 1930s movie actress Constance Bennett, charcoal with highlighting, done on a torn paper bag, 1972. Dan compares her to Botticelli in his note on the drawing. Collection of WTW.

Danny Allen, THE MANDRILL,
acrylic on board, 1973,
approximately 3 x 6 inches.
Collection of the Allen family.

I'M CONSTANTLY TORN ABOUT what to reveal and what to keep to myself about my years with Danny. At last I've decided to conceal as little as possible—perhaps only the things I have yet to reveal to myself—and when I do reveal them to myself, I promise to share them.

After Dan died, I entered a state of emotional suspended animation. Following a decent passage of time, I continued with my life as best I could, but I was numb.

Dan's suicide was different than the average death, which is bad enough. Something very unusual happens among those who know you when you're the surviving partner of a person who has taken his or her own life. Some people level blame at you, looking for answers wherever they can find them, be they right or wrong. Everyone in Dan's life had lost a beloved friend. We'd lost a talented young man whom we all expected to watch grow, develop, and thrive. Then there was nothing but sudden pain and unanswerable questions.

As the survivor, I found that people assumed I must somehow be at fault—if in no other way, then for the offense of still being alive. And it was hard for people to accept that Dan had left no note. Even with a note, however, there might not be a tangible explanation for an act in which the victim is the perpetrator—two people in one, taking their secrets with them to the grave.

That's not how the observers thought. This isn't what others wanted or expected to hear. And I felt it would be disloyal of me to articulate the two distinctly different sides to Dan's personality that I'd witnessed. So mostly I kept silent about what I knew.

As the survivor, I found that people demonized me, either directly or by way of giving me "attitude." They reinforced a silent suffering already well in progress. I'm not alone in having experienced this; I've spoken to other survivors of a partner's suicide, and they've expressed similar emotions. Even as you're experiencing the blame leveled at you by others, verbally or through subliminal glances, you remain your own worst accuser.

Danny Allen, watercolor of a self-mutilation, ca. 1973. Collection of WTW.

Thoughts ran through my mind constantly. What should I have done different-ly? Was there something I'd said or done that had enabled his self-destruction? What had I missed? Was I a terrible person? Should it have been me instead who'd died? The loss leads to a depression of circular self-recrimination. Worst of all is this grotesque question: Did he decide that it was better to be dead than to be alive and be my lover? All of this might sound irrational to a person who hasn't experienced what I have, but these are the confusing thoughts that possess a surviving partner's mind.

I knew that some people thought Dan had taken his life because our relation-ship was in trouble, but I think that he was destined to be on this earth only a very short time. Dan and I had discussed breaking up, but we hadn't done anything about it other than having the occasional argument. We remained together and made up after spats, only to have the pattern recycle itself. Had he not killed himself while with me, he would have done it at another time. However, knowing that doesn't stop me from feeling responsible.

A self-hatred set in that I came to terms with only by trying to understand that every individual is in control of his or her own decisions. This helps, but it's cold comfort that doesn't last long. Intellectually, the surviving partner knows that he or she is not at fault. Viscerally, though, I always believe secretly that somehow I was to blame. I was already blaming myself, so when other people blamed me, I absorbed it. I took it on. It became a part of me.

With Danny dead, I found it impossible to reconcile the different parts of him I'd known. Instead, I was left with my initial impressions of him—with how I'd defined him when we'd fallen in love. I'll call it blind denial, if that helps to convey my point. He was a brilliantly talented young man who seemed to know how to do everything he set out to accomplish.

The stories of those who lost Dan and continue to suffer are many. Dan's friend Ramon, a fellow painter, had been on the outs with Dan over a foolish difference of opinion, and Ramon spent the rest of his life regretting that he and Dan had parted while they were estranged. There was no chance to say goodbye, let alone to ask why. Sudden death heightens all of your emotions, and everything around you becomes both more vividly real and more unreal.

In time, I visited Danny's mother and father. I was driven to their home by a friend, probably Diana. I wanted Dan's parents to have his painting *The Mandrill* because it expressed the depth of his talent and astonishing technical expertise without dwelling on his personal demons. I didn't want his parents to suffer from Danny's personal demons. Their own pain was more than enough to bear. I wanted to give them another way to remember the goodness of Dan. As Dan wrote in his journal,

> *You know you exist in a permanent state of impermanency. And you know that nothing you may do will save you from mortality. Still, you hope to be remembered forever, but not the unremembered one.*

Even in death, Dan is nothing if not remembered for his distinctive behavior. Nancy Rosin remembers a time when the two of them were working in an old mansion on East Avenue. They'd been hired to strip off beautiful, intact antique wallpaper because someone thought it was dowdy and out of style, and they were feeling terrible about it. To cheer themselves up, Dan made Peter Pan hats out of large scraps of torn wallpaper, which they wore while carrying out their task.

If only Dan had valued himself more. But it seemed that Dan wanted to shed this life for the next. Most of us have a fear of the unknown; Dan was drawn to it. That said, there is nothing romantic about the unknown realm of suicide. And it's one hell of a destructive way to get people to remember you.

Before I moved—or should I say fled—to Philadelphia, I gave Dan's cat, Natasha Sweetmeat, to his mother, Mrs. Allen. Our other cat, Pushpin, had run away during all the confusion. I knew that Natasha would have a far better home with Dan's mother than she would with me in a cramped little apartment in metropolitan Philadelphia. Still, giving Natasha away was hard. I loved her, and she represented something gentle and living that had belonged to Dan. What I really wanted to do was to rip my heart out and give it to Danny's mother—to both of his parents. Dan was their first-born and his father's namesake. It was impossible not to realize the misery his parents were living in; everyone who'd loved Dan dearly was in a parallel personal hell. But there was no means at my disposal to make things right. We would all have to live with Dan's decision. At least Dan's mother could hold and love that cat, who lived out her life stalking the fields and shores of Lake Ontario, near Danny's family home.

Chronology isn't my strong suit, and it's also not the most important aspect of the story I'm trying to tell. One minute I'll have a recollection about the times after Dan died, and then another memory will bring him back to life again. There is much sadness and pain, but writing about the life I shared with Dan when he was still among the living is a comfort. And Rochester itself was a major source of fascination and amazement to me, as I believe it was to Dan as well. Anyone who could see Rochester through my eyes would be at a loss to disagree.

The year before a dollhouse I built was exhibited in Toronto, the Rochester Memorial Art Gallery had a special winter holiday exhibit—a huge installation of Victorian toys and dollhouses. Everything was on loan from the Margaret Woodbury Strong Museum. The Strong Museum collection was still in the late heiress's home then and was being viewed by the general public for the first time. I was invited to display one of my miniature houses opposite the gift shop, and in many ways it upstaged the more patinaed antiques from the Strong Museum's collection, which led to my being offered a second job: working on objects at the Strong.

Thereafter, my time was split between the Strong Museum, which was a lunatic asylum filled with toys and eccentric personalities, and the Rochester Memorial Art Gallery, which was populated by fascinating, erudite drunkards.

Bill Whiting, Tudor dollhouse, 1 inch = 1 foot scale, ca. 1972. Collection of the Toy and Miniature Museum of Kansas City.

If memory serves me, the Strong Museum had 641 dollhouses and approximately thirty thousand dolls—a startling number of which were in need of some sort of repair or paint touch-up. So I had a brilliant idea. I told them that I needed assistance repairing painted finishes on artifacts, and Dan was the perfect choice. Dan was much better at restoring paint, while I was better at carving replacement parts. For a while we both had bicycles, until one got stolen; weather permitting, on days when we were both working there, we'd peddle the long ride to the museum, which was outside the city limits, to "paint smiles on dolls," as Dan put it. If it snowed, other employees would give us a lift out to the museum and back.

In the twenty-first century, the Strong Museum might not be very happy with what I'm about to reveal, but truth be told, back then the administration kept very sloppy records. I suspect that some of the people in high places were finding creative ways of liberating funds from the museum's coffers. They were also asking Dan and me to over-restore artifacts to mint condition, with no one in charge of keeping professional records of those alterations. In the museum world, that's not considered ethical practice. But Danny and I were clueless.

I went to the Strong Museum two days a week to repair dolls and dollhouses to pristine condition, sometimes with Dan, and sometimes alone. As those repairs were completed, pieces that had been in fair condition were listed in their records as being in mint condition. Thus we were the unwitting accomplices to these false increases in the value of certain artifacts, while we earned fractions of a penny on an object's alleged worth. Not only were the improvements dishonest unless duly recorded as alterations, but some items didn't really benefit from their makeovers; some dollhouses in the collection that the curator wanted repainted or redecorated should never have been touched. It's frowned on not to preserve original paint. Dan restored the paint on some rare mechanized iron banks, and to prove how heavily they'd been restored, one would require a paint analysis—that's how convincing his work was. In a contemporary museum setting, modifications like that would be carefully documented and photographed in stages if deemed ethical and necessary.

But the Strong was not a tightly run ship. One by one, the top brass of the museum were either caught with their hands in the cookie jar or caught using their museum credentials to purchase pieces for their own collections, which led to them being ousted in disgrace. The place was a managerial mess, to the point that it was difficult for me to know to whom I answered toward the end of my career there. That museum was Rochester's pièce de résistance of bizarre eccentricity. While it was still being organized in Mrs. Strong's mansion, it made all of Rochester's other crazies pale in comparison.

The collection's origins are interesting to note. Rochester boasted many booming industries over the years, and Margaret Strong's father had owned a very successful riding-crop and horse-supply company that had been founded in the nineteenth century. Her father gave George Eastman a small business loan and thus left Margaret an inheritance that included 51 percent of Eastman Kodak, back when Kodak stock was worth something.

Margaret Strong was a very odd, reclusive woman who died the year I moved to Rochester, so I never got to meet her. She'd lived in an Italianate, Gatsby-style mansion at the end of a winding, mile-long lane graced with decorative bridges, mallard ponds, and garden whimsies. Topsy-turvy topiary trees in sorrowful neglect greeted you as you made your way down the driveway to the mansion. Those sad, sculptural trees had once resembled things like giraffes and giant frogs but were in a pitiful state of neglect. Unpruned branches sprang from the plants, giving the animals extra tails and antlers in the most unlikely places. Dan, of course, loved them exactly the way they were. On warm days, the two of us would sit outside by the topiary trees, eating our brown-bag lunches and discussing what kinds of creatures these animals would morph into, if left further unattended.

On our way to work, we'd make it down the driveway, then approach the museum through an outdoor path of electrified gnome villages populated with tiny houses, roads, and street lamps, all of which were lower than knee height; everything about the place was off-the-charts abnormal. We entered the main house through an atrium, and once inside, we'd pass glassy-eyed interns—one group on the left of the entrance, and one group on the right. Both sets were sorting through gigantic refrigerator boxes full of buttons. One box was filled with black glass "jet-bead" buttons. The other was filled with white, mother-of-pearl buttons. These poor interns were burdened with the insufferable task of matching beads and buttons into sets and pulling out buttons that might contain diamonds, pearls, or semiprecious stones—and then of storing sets in little plastic bags and assigning everything accession numbers. No madhouse in the world could have been more dreamlike or unsettling. Dan and I were fascinated.

Then there were the dolls. Mrs. Strong's collection of dolls went way beyond the obsessive and right into the compulsive. There was a peculiar addition to the house, built onto the side, that cascaded down the hill. The addition ruined the stately proportions of the mansion, as if a junior-high school or a low-income housing project had been slapped onto this multimillion-dollar estate. But Mrs. Strong had had the addition built to store dolls and dollhouses, watchmaker's journeyman pieces, and peculiar examples of American popular culture spanning the preceding two hundred years.

She got an early start with her extraordinary collection. As a child, she was taken on trips all over the world, and everywhere she visited, her parents sent her out with her nanny and a good-sized carpetbag. Margaret was told she could buy anything she wanted, just so long as it fit inside the bag. Good things, as they say, come in small packages, and thus Margaret Strong was introduced to minutiae. Imagine a child traveling through pre-Boxer Rebellion China, set loose in shops and marketplaces, given free range to decide what she bought.

Once when Danny and I were perusing the collection, we found German bisque dolls that were anatomically correct to an alarming degree of erotic detail, and rare French fashion dolls, and dolls with creepy smiles that showed sharp white teeth—not to mention wooden Queen Anne dolls, Fanny Brice dolls, and dolls from the Orient that were made up like Kabuki actors. We also discovered some items that were definitely one of a kind, including a peanut shell with pipe-cleaner arms and legs that was wearing a tutu and sporting a tiny blonde wig, with a picture of Nancy Sinatra's face glued to the front of the shell. We both nearly collapsed to the floor and laughed until we had to pee.

As we walked through the house, room after room of glassy-eyed doll people glared out from the locked glass shelves that lined the endless corridors. I regret never having gone there stoned, but it was enough of a trip simply to be there sober.

Bill Whiting, Tudor dollhouse,
1 inch = 1 foot scale,
still under construction in 1972.
Collection of the Toy and Miniature
Museum of Kansas City.

There were even oddities beneath the floor. The mansion had once housed a small indoor pool, which at some point had been covered with flooring. When the flooring was removed, everyone present was dismayed to discover that the pool was filled to the brim with bits of dolls and toys—arms, legs, heads, little hands, glass eyes, miniature dresses, wigs, and bicycle wheels. How on earth had this come to be? We could only wonder. This place was not any kind of normal, not by any of the standards I've seen before or since. It merits mentioning that Rod Serling, creator of the *Twilight Zone*, was from Rochester. This makes perfect sense.

Given all the doll amputees lying around, of course there were still more glazed-eyed interns attempting to match missing arms and legs to doll bodies. Once a score was made, Dan and I would reconstruct the doll and fix the paint, and I'd carve or recreate whatever part or parts couldn't be located. We'd walk into my workroom to find notes attached to large boxes—notes written by the poor, exhausted, overworked registrar—that outlined our instructions for the day. I remember my favorite note, which read: "Turtles of all descriptions, mostly wearing kilts, some containing golf bags full of swizzle-sticks. Repair what you can. I'm going home. I have a migraine." Who could doubt her?

There must have been something in the tap water in upstate New York. Its history of weirdness runs mighty and deep. In the 1800s, the Rochester area was a breeding ground for crackpot religions and far-out spirituality. For example, the Fox sisters lived in Rochester in the nineteenth century. They were faith healers (scammers, really) who communicated messages they received from the dead by loudly cracking their fingers and toes. This was certainly a unique way of communicating with the hereafter. They'd interpret the cracking noises as messages from deceased relatives to churches and auditoriums packed with anyone gullible enough to believe them. Of course the sisters racked up a small fortune and later recanted their claims, admitting to being frauds, before they died. There's a bronze statue of the Fox Sisters in Cornhill, near the Campbell Whittlesey House, a couple of blocks from the carriage house on Greenwood Street—if the statue still stands. What am I thinking? Of course it does. It must weigh five thousand pounds.

Take the Mormons for another example of Rochester's fascinating strangeness. The Mormon faith originally began as a nineteenth-century polygamy cult, cooked up by a grifter named Joe Smith just southeast of Rochester on Hill Cumorah in Palmyra, New York. Dan used to take me and a bunch of friends to the annual Mormon Pageant each year. We'd get high on pot or hash brownies before we parked the car, and we'd smuggle in jug wine under Diana's extra-large Indian-print skirt. Thus loaded, we'd witness a very peculiar religious musical, complete with a recording of the Mormon Tabernacle Choir that boomed over the loudspeakers. The highlights of the performance included bleating sheep, what appeared to be Viking ships, and uplighted sets of the archeologically unfounded Seven Lost Cities of Gold. All kinds of trippy stuff took place on stage, none of which seemed to make a lick of sense. I'm proud to admit that I lay with Dan on a blanket under the stars and made out while the Angel Moroni made his theatrical descent to deliver the "Word of God" to Joseph Smith. How many gay men can say a thing like that? Talk about Boni-Moroni.

I still remember Diana the Witch losing control, laughing until she had the hiccups, when the sound of bleating sheep came across the P.A. system, blended with the musical stylings of the Mormon Tabernacle Choir. Once Diana got laughing, Dan got laughing, which then got me going, until we were told to settle down or leave. Like bad kids reprimanded for cutting up in the back of the bus, we continued to misbehave, only more quietly. The entire thing made about as much sense as a musical production of *Lord of the Rings* performed backwards in Coptic. Think HOBBIT! *The Musical* and you kind of get the picture.

My years living with Dan in Rochester redefined my definition of peculiarity forever. But we weren't, any of us, wrapped too tightly ourselves.

Danny Allen, paper collage, ca. 1970.
Collection of Nancy Rosin.

Diana even held séances and spiritual rituals in historic Mount Hope Cemetery, though these gatherings were more like poorly thought-out performance-art experiments. Stones, sticks, and feathers might be arranged on a boulder, tombstone, or tree stump. Diana would chant, doing her level best to make contact with the world beyond the flesh. People milled about with lighted candles, pretending to spook each other, high as kites. Nothing came of it aside from the wind stirring and Diana saying, "Did you hear that noise?" or "Did you see that light from behind the trees?" Eventually the pot would leave everyone hungry, and a whole mess of people would land at Mama Tacconi's all-night pizzeria, or whatever all-night diner would serve a motley gaggle of stoned hippies with the munchies.

Mama Tacconi's food wasn't much to write home about, but you'd have thought it was the best Italian cuisine in the world from the way she strutted about. She would sit on her throne-like chair, which was raised on a platform, in her apron covered with spaghetti sauce, surveying her patrons while they ate. One night we ordered steamed clams, and when they arrived unopened we flagged our server, but Mama Tacconi herself swooped down on us, incensed that anyone would find fault with her food. We told her the clams weren't open, which is a sign that they're not safe to eat. Mama Tacconi scooped a clam out of the bowl, cracked it open with her teeth, ate it, and said, "You commah backa tomorrow and see if I'ma dead." Where upon Diana the Witch replied, "I won't need to come back, I'll already know. I'm in regular contact with the dead." Mama Tacconi wouldn't even comp our meal. I never heard if she got sick from the clam, though she looked like she had an indestructible constitution.

Danny knew about food. He was a good cook and had his own culinary interests. He also seemed to be the salt in our collective stew, the ingredient that kept our odd group of friends together as a unit.

POEM #54

When it's time to eat chicken you know
you're over twenty five in body, mind and spirit.
Chicken is fine fried so get the gasses burning.
Hot vapor from a tongue of boiling water.
The pot never boils if it is watched too closely,
so pay no attention and it will do the inevitable.
They put what's to cook inside.
I love my lobster hot and juicy.

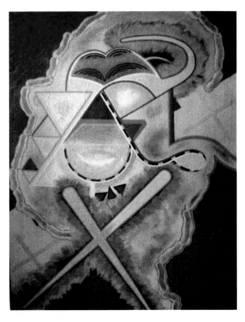

Danny Allen, nonobjective piece, acrylic on canvas, ca. 1968.
Collection of the Allen family.

ARTISTS ARE BORN NONCONFORMISTS. While other children
were drawing stick figures, Danny's childhood art resembled sophisticated
American primitive paintings rather than the doodlings of a child. Even in
the piece pictured on the next page, the tree and fence are decidedly in the
foreground. The house with the waterwheel, while anchoring the picture, is
offset by the suggestion of trees in the distance. Dan was born with a sense
of composition, the gift of observation, and absolutely no fear of color whatsoever. I don't think there was ever any question that Danny was born with
creativity flowing through his veins.

Danny Allen, crayon drawing done when Dan was no more than ten years old. Collection of the Allen family.

Danny Allen, opaque watercolor, painted in 1958, when Dan was twelve years old. Collection of the Allen family.

While creative people are growing and experiencing the world that surrounds us, we come naturally to question authority. The generation to which Dan and I belonged also benefited from the struggles and sacrifices made by the generations that preceded us; we took for granted the warm homes we lived in and the food on our tables, just as many young people do today. Yet through our heightened senses, creative people perceived things that didn't make sense to us. We rebelled, and our rebellion unsettled the older generation, who'd lived through the Great Depression and World War II.

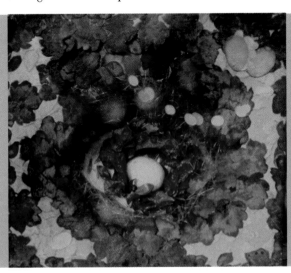

*Danny Allen,
three-dimensional
shadowbox collage,
ca. 1965.
Collection of the
Allen family.*

Dan was my lover, but of course he was far more than that. He was a son and a brother, a loved little boy and a hopeful youth. His death sent shock waves through everyone he touched. Our friend Gary is someone to whom people often tell their deepest feelings. He recalled a private conversation with Dan from which he came away with complete certainty that Dan loved his family and adored his brothers and sisters. After Dan died, Gary wrote a letter to Mrs. Allen, telling her about that conversation. Having never seen Gary before in her life, Mrs. Allen picked him out of the crowd at the funeral service and walked up to thank him. "You're the young man who wrote me that beautiful letter," she said.

Being the oldest of the Allen children, Dan was naturally the first to launch out on his own, but he took the time to do portraits of his younger siblings, portraits that now have an irreplaceable hold on the family's collective heart.

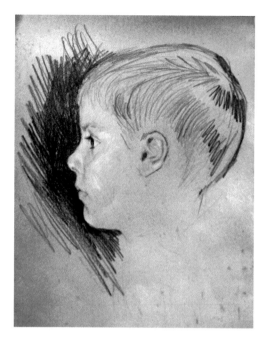

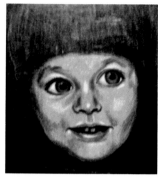

Danny Allen, portraits of his brother Robert, left, and his sister Christine, above, both charcoal with highlighting, 1968. Collection of the Allen family.

Dan's youngest sister, Christine, was nine when he died. Knowing how I would value seeing these pieces, she sent me copies of Dan's earliest childhood art. These early expressions of a budding talent go beyond stereotypical childhood art. To me, the most touching and poignant artworks of Danny's remain those he created in childhood. No doubt these works will always be cherished by the Allen family; his childhood art presents a concrete sense of the Danny they knew.

Dan was loved because he was lovable. When I knew him, he was also lovable because he was troubled. You might not have been able to put your finger on the word *troubled* or to recognize what was brewing inside him, but his personality was hypnotic. Dan was a house on fire, but everyone around him felt only the warmth.

All did not always go smoothly at home with the oldest Allen child. Dan's brother Lee remembers their dad ordering Dan to cut his shoulder-length hair when he was young. No son of his was going to be a hippie. The parental generation of the 1960s was completely flummoxed by their children's actions—growing long hair and beards, attending peace protests, not adhering to the mold they were expected to fit into. On that particular day, after a period of

Danny Allen, portraits of family friends, the Lowden family, charcoal with highlighting. Collection of the Lowden family.

flared tempers, Dan locked himself in the bathroom and shaved his head. That was the end of that. The hair grew back, and Dan kept it long. As I understand it, their father never mentioned the length of Dan's hair again.

Our generation was rebellious. We rebelled against stereotypes. We rebelled against the Vietnam War. We rallied around music that taught us to pursue peace, without grasping how unlikely it was for the world to be receptive to or tolerant of these ideas.

Recently I had a wonderful telephone conversation with Dan's sister Jackie, who is two years younger than Dan. We shared our recollections of her brother, filling in gaps in each other's knowledge. For instance, I had known that Danny had dropped out of college at the Fashion Institute of Technology in New York, but I'd never known why. Apparently, he'd made his first suicide attempt there, a drug overdose. Danny's dad, a World War II Air Force veteran, most likely applied the conventional wisdom of the day to this crisis: he urged Dan to join the service, believing this would straighten Dan out and make a man of him. Like his father before him, Danny joined the Air Force.

Danny Allen,
watercolor of mallards, 1958.
Collection of the Allen family.

But Dan wasn't there for very long. He fell in love with his heterosexual bunk-mate, and the emotions tormented him so badly that he finally came out to his superior officers and was discharged. No wonder Dan didn't like to talk about his time in the Air Force. Not only did I not know about it until recently, but some of Dan's siblings only learned about it relatively recently themselves.

Another piece of conventional wisdom from those days to which we should no longer adhere is that people who attempt suicide are merely seeking atten-tion. Yes, to a certain degree, but I'd say more that their action is a cry for help. Suicide attempts are decidedly a sign of mental illness, and mental illness has always been misunderstood and stigmatized. I've seen mental illness in my own family and witnessed it handled with silent denial—as if to ignore the disease was the best way to make it go away.

Dan didn't tell me about his time in the Air Force, but he did tell me about clashes with his parents. Almost all young people go through an acrimonious phase with their parents—and sadly, by taking his own life, Dan never got to reconcile those feelings the way others of us have. This must have been dif-ficult for his parents, too. Danny's father was never anything other than

Danny Allen,
graphite drawing on cardboard,
approximately 10 x 12 inches.
Collection of the Allen family.

gracious and kind toward me. His dad is now gone, but I hope he understood that Danny's decisions belonged to Dan. I love Dan's mom, Bernice Allen, and I know that, as a devout Catholic, she has struggled to come to terms with how her son died.

Bernice told her surviving children that Dan was taken to see psychiatrists and doctors after many traumatic clashes between him and his parents, and that he was diagnosed as having severe mental problems on which I'm not qualified to elaborate. But Eva Weiss explained it to me in this way: "Once we had a box of cereal in front of us, and he was explaining that he didn't see things the way most of us do. I would see letters and numbers written on the side of the box, and Dan would see objects turning into figures or numbers turning into other things. I never questioned it, as it was all a part of who he was, and it all came out in his art. And then there were the kind of drugs he preferred, which caused hallucinations."

Jackie told me something else that fascinated me: that the Allen children come from a long line of artists dating back generations. Jackie also told me that her older brother always made her feel beautiful. They often played together, and sometimes he would dress her up like a doll. She recalled him fixing her hair into a French twist and doing her make-up before her junior prom. Jackie sat down for her makeover as a little girl and met her date looking like she belonged on the cover of a magazine. She still keeps a series of handmade, emerald-green bows that Danny sewed to keep her French twist in place. There are distinct advantages to having a gay older brother with a natural sense of style.

She remembers Dan taking a pad of newsprint paper and dashing off sketch after sketch of fashion designs while she watched with fascination. Then he would crumple up drawings that other people would have saved. That interest in fashion led him to attend FIT, but apparently he wasn't cut out for that particular discipline. We'll never know what drove him to his first suicide attempt, but afterward he was sent home during the height of the Vietnam War.

Young men of draft age had very few options then. I remember the terror we all felt about the possibility of being drafted. I had a college deferment and was young enough that I pulled a high "lottery number" after the draft system was modified. Dan had no such options. Mental illness wasn't discussed, and Danny had a gift for hiding his troubled mind even from those closest to him. I've wondered why Dan didn't hop the border into Canada like so many other guys his age did. Perhaps he feared his father's disappointment. Or perhaps he viewed war as an honorable way to die.

But once freed from the constraints of college and the military, Dan was set loose to be the artist and hippie he wanted to be. He moved out to San Francisco, where, according to former roommate Greg, Dan was shocked by the gay promiscuity. I know, however, that over time he came to embrace it.

At one point during his time in San Francisco, Dan had a lover named Nathan, who became a Hare Krishna. Dan found that off-putting and they broke up. Danny then came down with hepatitis B and hitched a ride home to Rochester so Diana the Witch could look after him, which is where my history with him began.

But long before I ever met Danny, there were good times in his childhood home. His dad worked at Eastman Kodak, and the family made home movies with costumes and art direction by one Daniel Arthur Allen. To this day, those films are shown at some family gatherings, and a collective sigh of love, grief and adoration ricochets through the hearts of those who knew him. To his younger family members, Dan is a part of a baffling family legend.

When Dan and his brother Lee were little boys, they shared a bedroom, as the family was seven children large. Dan was a quiet and gentle older brother who kept his own counsel, while Lee was more boisterous and enjoyed rough-and-tumble sports. Dan excelled at swimming and ice-skating but was never as sports minded as Lee. Well liked in school, Dan was even voted senior class president, and of course he won "most artistic" and was listed as such in the school yearbook. Lee, like all of us, found his brother to be quiet, introspective, and not easy to read. But while he was growing up, Dan demonstrated a fearlessness that stunned the local kids.

The Allen family lived in a rural area near Lake Ontario. Dan, his siblings, and the neighboring children would gather at a farmer's barn each year to celebrate after the hay was harvested. The kids would pull together a gigantic pile of hay and climb the side of the barn, which had hoisting beams at each floor level that were used to transport items into the barn through pulleys and ropes. Most of the kids would climb to the first-story beam and dare each other to jump into the hay, which everyone thought was thrilling. The braver older kids would go to the second-story beam and leap into the hay. Dan, however, would climb all the way up to the third-story hoisting beam, which effectively placed him on the barn's roof, and would then fearlessly jump three stories in the air into that pile of hay. None of the other children would even consider doing that.

Remember how, when you were small, time seemed infinite? How snowfalls came up to your waist? Remember what it was like to believe that the world was built on hope and dreams and that life lasted forever? I'm trying to, as I look at Dan's childhood art. I'll admit: they break my heart more than all the other works combined.

UNTITLED POEM #46

Death probe kill chose.
Depth charge too shows.
A stranger took a leap.
Where those will lease.

A peek into cheese.
And leave the
haggard border hem.

Danny Allen.
preliminary sketch
and two graphite drawings.
Collection of Leah Warnick.

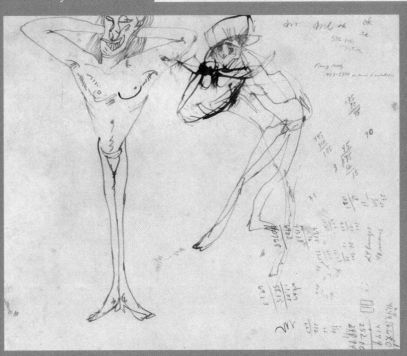

Danny Allen,
two collages,
paper, ca. 1970.
Collection of WTW.

MY LIFE WITH DANNY was several generations ago. I'm sixty-two years old as I write this, but I feel much older. I've led so many different lives that I have to reach back beyond miles of memories to recall how I felt when I was young. But I recall distinctly that when I first became Dan's lover, I looked up to him as my protector. There was a four-year difference between us, which made my inexperienced self consider him worldlier than he really was. I actually thought of Dan as an older man, but he was merely a boy. We're all still children when we're in our twenties, whether we know it or not.

Dan had the ability to make me feel special and desirable. I wanted and needed that in my life. When I lost it, I became empty. I tried to mold other men I met into facsimiles of the best qualities of Dan—which is entirely unfair to another person.

But what I had experienced with Dan was so precious to me that I found life without it desperate and awful. New love, especially when it's the first love, is different from any other kind. And making love with Dan was comfortable. Looking back on my awkward fumblings with other guys, I see that when I first came out, it was anything but comfortable. Even when we weren't making love, Dan and I felt the presence of love when we worked together in our studio. We didn't need to be saying anything to be communicating. We were working, each in his own world, together while alone with our thoughts.

That was different for me. I've never been the kind of artist who wanted other people looking over my shoulder while I worked. But when Dan did it, it was fine with me. If he offered suggestions or criticism, I recognized a validity in his words that I embraced and took to heart. I was never able to replicate that simpatico again. After I lost Dan, another young man I lived with briefly was so bored by pretending to enjoy working on drawings in the studio while I carved at my worktable that he finally said to me, "You know I'll never be Danny Allen." He got up and went out to a bar—alone.

For the remainder of my life, I've only waded into the shallow end of the emotional pool of relationships. Consciously or subconsciously, I've chosen people who could never love me. Doing that creates the illusion of feeling something without facing any genuine emotional risk. I've had relationships with people who have needed me, but I've positioned myself in a guardian role, which kept me at a safe distance: That way, I could convince myself that I didn't need anyone in return.

I could argue that losing Dan set my life on a solitary path, but I can't blame him for my solitude. I've had a lot of time to rebuild my emotional life and have not chosen to do so. I've done everything in my power to keep love better than an arm's length away. Hopefully we get wiser as we get older, but knowing something doesn't mean we know how to change it. I'm set in my ways now, and it's a beat too late to matter anymore. The loss of Danny left me terrified of any and all intimacy. I've lived decades with an ache behind what I'm told is my solar plexus. That ache doesn't happen as much as it used to, but I've groomed myself for solitude and even resent interruptions to my time alone.

One thing I learned about myself with Dan is that I'm inclined toward imprinting my personality on houses and apartments, leaving no room whatsoever for my partners to express their own personalities. When Dan and I lived on Merriman Street, I became so anal about keeping our apartment the way I wanted it that I got us to move our art studio to the abandoned basement of the house. That way, my overbearing presence was featured against a backdrop of pristine interior decoration, without the mess that making art creates. This dirt-floor, basement studio was fine for me; I was cutting wood and building miniature houses. But Dan was working on drawings and paintings that required natural light and clean surfaces. Putting our studio in the basement remains one of the worst things on my conscience when I look back at our life together.

Fortunately, that period of basement banishment lasted only a short period. One day I walked in to find Danny sitting in the basement with tears in his eyes. The space reminded him too much of Diana's basement, and he hated it. I hated myself for having imposed my foolish will. Together, we returned

Stephen Plunkett, photo of Dan Allen.

*Stephen Plunkett,
photo of Dan Allen with
another model.*

Stephen Plunkett, photo of Dan Allen.

Stephen Plunkett,
photo of Dan Allen
with another model.

Stephen Plunkett, photo of Dan Allen.

the studio to where it belonged, in the middle of our attic apartment, and we agreed that Dan should have the corner with the window and the northern light.

At the beginning of our relationship, Dan had appeared to be the stronger personality of the two of us. But as I brought home the steady paycheck, my role changed. Slowly, almost imperceptibly, I took the upper hand. The new dynamic happened so subtly neither of us was fully aware of our switched roles. I didn't have any better idea of what we were doing than Dan did—but we were doing it.

Someone I recently corresponded with, someone far more knowledgeable than I am concerning the human psyche, proposed a theory about Dan that briefly upended my world. Dan was every bit a man and generously endowed as such. But the body isn't the soul of a human being. It was suggested to me that Dan's inner conflict might have been caused by his body being male and his psychological gender assignment being female. That implies more than mere homosexuality; it suggests that Dan, who was not particularly effeminate, might have been psychologically female in a male body. At first I was upset by the theory. When I took a closer look at Danny's drawings of transgendered, hermaphroditic figures, I saw the theory's merit, but I remain skeptical. Yet as I considered this possibility, I felt a new insecurity. If Dan was psycho-

logically female, did that mean he'd never really loved me? I had to shake that illogical insecurity out of my thoughts and move on. The sad reality is that he disliked himself more than he loved me; that much is clear. As to Danny's psychological gender assignment, no one will ever know. But his inner demons might have been hiding right in his artwork, in plain sight. Transgendered people were very rare in those days and suffered even worse discrimination than they do today. It has never been an easy life path.

But there was far more to Danny than demons. He and I could play like children, even though we were supposedly grown men. We would even play with the dollhouses I built. I rarely let anyone touch them, but Danny had carte blanche.

One day, as I entered our Merriman Street apartment, he asked me to sit down.

While he and I sat in the kitchen, drinking cups of something awful like Tang, he said to me, "You've got to try this new weed I got." He drew on a joint, then handed it over to me. "I've got a surprise for you," he continued, "but you need to get really, really stoned to appreciate it." I took in another deep toke, choking out the smoke, burning my throat. The stuff has always made me cough.

But Danny was overflowing with energy and had mischievous bedevilment in his eyes. When he decided we were good and high, he told me to close my eyes, and he led me into the studio. When I opened my eyes, I was looking into the back of an elaborate Tudor dollhouse I'd built. Dan had taken museum wax and completely redecorated the dollhouse so that all the furniture was neatly arranged on the ceilings. He'd created a miniature Jean Cocteau moment for me.

Dan took off his pants and opened the front door of the dollhouse so he could stick his penis through the door. He had a little plastic cowgirl doll he'd named Sally, and she was riding him like a bucking bronco, exploding through the front door, with the furniture hanging from the ceiling. We took Polaroids that I wish I still had in my possession.

Bill Whiting, interior room of Tudor dollhouse, 1 inch = 1 foot scale.
Collection of the Toy and Miniature Museum of Kansas City.

Pulling some of the furniture down, we took turns photographing our junk on miniature beds and sofas, forcing them through doors or draping them over tables and chairs. It's amazing how big your dick looks when it's draped over a miniature doll chair. We giggled and kissed and went to our life-sized bed, only to reemerge a while later to discover how difficult it was to remove museum wax from tiny decorative ceilings. If I'd done that with anyone other than Dan, I would have been furious about the mess and inevitable clean-up. But we got it cleaned up, and that dollhouse is now in an important museum collection and has been exhibited around the world. In my opinion, our antics only add value to the piece.

Bill Whiting, miniature chairs.
Collection of WTW

Bill Whiting, miniature Empire chair,
1 inch = 1 foot scale.
Collection of Jean and Carleen Gazabat.

I could never be entirely certain what was going to come out of Dan's mouth. One night, while making love, he became angry and accusatory with me, claiming that our passion was so intense because I was thinking about someone else. I hadn't called out anyone else's name. There wasn't anyone else; there didn't need to be. But Dan had made up his mind that there was. Looking back, I see that Dan had been jealous of a fellow named Scott, who'd worked with me at Sibley's.

Scott knew he was hot, and he displayed his cockiness in distinctive and absurd ways. He'd pull his pants down in front of me when we were alone in the elevators, just to pluck my nerves, and then he'd be all zipped up and tucked in

Danny Allen, sepia ink on newsprint, 1973. Collection of WTW.

before the elevator stopped at the next floor to pick up store customers. I'd be a total wreck, as much out of fear of being fired over something I hadn't instigated as from the sight of Scott's well-muscled exhibitionism. But I never did anything with him. Scott's thing was to flirt with people and to be admired and desired. But that night in bed, Dan argued that I had to have been thinking about someone else, and he got it into his head that it was Scott.

Right then, out of nowhere as far as I was concerned, Danny demanded that we have an open relationship. I was in love with Dan, and until moments before, I'd been making love with Dan. But now the rules included making love with other people. Dan got dressed and went out into the night by himself.

I lay awake all night and heard him come in. I was so dense that I had to have him spell out what an open relationship meant. Internally, I took it to mean that Danny was bored with me and wanted variety and that he'd gone about asking for it by accusing me of thinking about what he was already doing. These are the mind games that tear at the fabric of a relationship.

Danny Allen. PLEASE BE SEATED. *watercolor, 1972. Collection of WTW.*

Dan could be accusatory without apparent reason. He once instigated an argument when the wind slammed a door shut; he accused me of slamming the door on purpose to break his concentration. I told him the wind had done it. I wasn't anywhere near the door. But by that point, it didn't matter how the door had gotten slammed. We had a senseless argument well underway, with both of us making it worse.

Even before Dan had demanded an open relationship, I knew that he played around. He always had. It stung (especially the gonorrhea), and it made me fear that I wasn't enough to satisfy Dan's needs, sexually or emotionally.

Now, as an older man, I understand the role that sexual variety can play in the real and fantasy sex lives of all men, gender assignment notwithstanding. But back then, from my perspective, our new love had slowly morphed into uncomfortable love. I felt that I was less than what I was expected to be. This made me willing to try things I wouldn't have otherwise done. We tried a three-way once with someone Dan picked up, and I was completely out of step with the groove, so to speak. I felt left out at the same time as I was being pulled in. At heart, I was still a sheltered suburban kid who only looked like a hippie. I was abysmally un-hip. I'm compelled to cast myself in the role of the host: "Can I get you boys anything? Coffee? Tea? Condoms?" But I'm being facetious; no one gave a thought to condoms back then. The AIDS epidemic was less than a decade away, but no one worried about sexually transmitted diseases. You got a shot or a pill or a cream and jumped right back into the game.

Little by little, Dan and I fell into a pattern of separate one-night stands—brief, dirty little encounters that didn't matter and that were rarely repeated with the same stranger. Danny and I didn't talk about it, unless it involved a trip to the clinic. I remember being with a guy named Will, a guy named Tommy, and a fellow named John, who later became a friend—but I wasn't all that good at picking up guys. Dan had it down to a science. I always knew when he'd been with someone else, because he'd be noticeably less affectionate toward me and would shower almost the minute he entered the apartment.

An open relationship might work for some people, but it never worked for me. It threw off our sexual time clock as a couple. It also left me feeling less valued, less loved, and more confused about everything. I don't know how it made Dan feel, but it was his house rule. I seemed to rule over everything else—the practical stuff, that is.

When a couple falls into a volley of outside indiscretions, feelings get hurt. Retributions beg to play themselves out, without either partner being wise to the game they're playing. Our arguments led to things being said that neither of us meant, and the topic of breaking up would surface, only to be later solved in the bedroom. As I noted earlier, when a man asks for an open relationship, he doesn't really expect his partner to take him up on it. I'm of the mind that the request is subconsciously a one-sided expectation. For the most part it was with Dan, because I've never been particularly skilled at connecting sexually with strangers.

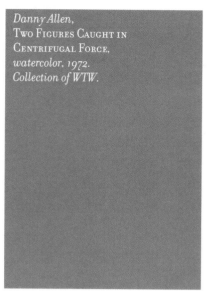

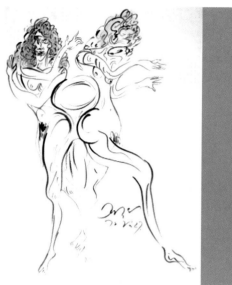

Danny Allen,
TWO FIGURES CAUGHT IN
CENTRIFUGAL FORCE,
watercolor, 1972.
Collection of WTW.

Before long, Dan and I had separate bedrooms. I'd decorated one for myself in a way that was very, very telling. It had white walls, a white floor, and a white trellis gazebo bed in the middle of a room, with no other furniture. It was the textbook definition of an iceberg. It photographed beautifully, but it wasn't really a room—it was an installation. I'd get up in the middle of the night and go to Dan's bed, feeling cold and not wanting to be alone. On those nights, we would make love as if a stranger had entered the bedroom, uninvited and

unexpected. It was the best way I had at my disposal to be the stranger Dan craved. Perhaps it was the best way for me to have that stranger, too.

I've thought a lot about what makes a relationship fall to pieces. Hurt feelings. Insecurity. A lack of honest communication—and a failure to know when to bend to the will of the other and when to enforce your own stand.

Danny Allen, watercolor, 1974.
Collection of WTW.

Danny Allen, India ink on bond, ca. 1974, Collection of WTW.

It's all that and probably much more. The less you understand yourself and your partner, the more love hurts. We had intensity without open understanding. The love wasn't gone, but it went into hiding, and I didn't feel safe or secure in our relationship.

The next thing I knew, we had arguments about everything and anything, except what was really on our minds. Love falls apart not because neither party is talking, but because both lovers are talking about anything except the heart of the matter. And so it was with Dan and me.

An elderly woman once asked me, "After all these years, are you still in love with Danny because he killed himself?" It's a fair question—a brutal one, but fair. However, I don't think that's the case. For all that happened, for all that went catastrophically wrong, I miss Dan. No one ever made me feel the way he did, good or bad.

That said, if you want to get revenge on someone and live under their skin for the rest of their days, take your life. I don't recommend it, and for those who have done it, I'm certain they had no idea how many people would be left in their wake, suffering in endless pain.

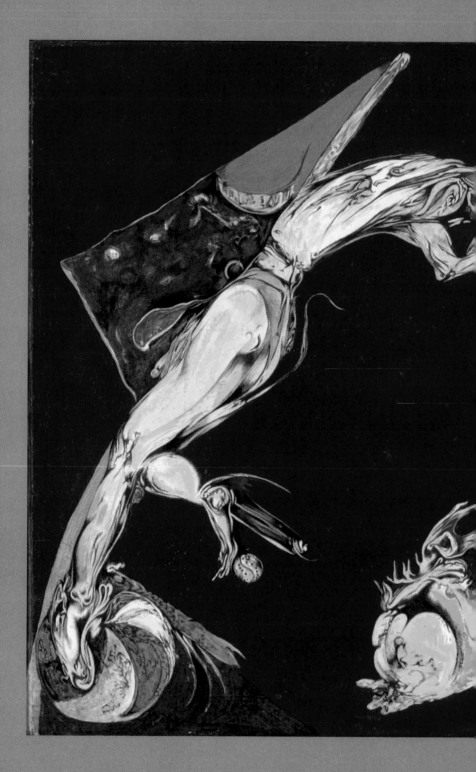

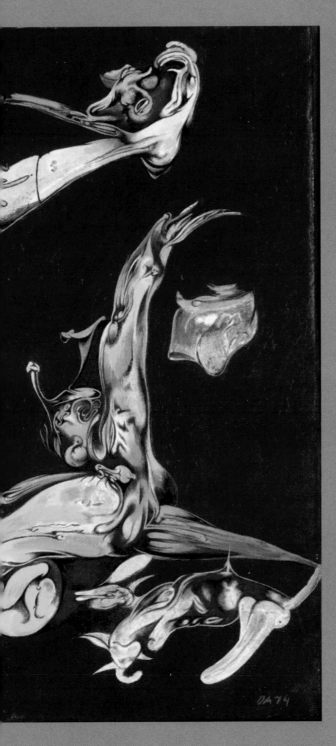

Danny Allen,
acrylic on paper
decoupaged to canvas.
1974.
Collection of
Albert Robbins.

Danny Allen, India ink sketch, 1973. Collection of WTW.

After Dan died, emotional erosion took hold of me, redefining love as emotional pain—pain I was determined never to experience again. I was stalled in a holding pattern of nonstop hurt. I suspect that I came of age already burdened with a strong fear of intimacy. After Dan died, I perfected that fear, building impenetrable emotional walls around myself. I could love my friends, adore my pets, and care deeply about any number of people and things—but I withdrew from partnered love, save for a few unsuccessful attempts that only reinforced my opinions. I intentionally undermined all my romantic efforts, only to deceive myself into believing I was rebuilding my life, one failed relationship at a time. The only thing I came away with was a talent for being alone and for accepting the appearance of contentment.

A lot of years have passed. I've thought a great deal about all that happened and have reflected on Dan's question to me: "If I take my life, will you follow me?" The truth is that, while I didn't follow him off the bridge, my life has followed his death in ways he could never have imagined, perhaps in ways far more profound than a shared suicide. I have shared my life with Dan's death.

Danny Allen, shadowbox assemblage, ca. 1970. Whereabouts and ownership unknown.

BEST AS I CAN RECALL, the sun only shines in Rochester, New York, when someone is considering moving there, at which time the town is gorgeous. But that isn't quite fair to say, because it is a beautiful city, with a gray, unpredictable sky and winds that blow down from the north with no warning.

Once Danny and I had a powerful encounter with those unpredictable winds. We rode our bicycles all the way to Lake Ontario during a midwinter thaw one January. It must have been at least 72 degrees outside. Foolish as we were, we decided that spring was coming early. We took off our shirts and lay in the sun by the lake. The sun was warm, though the breeze was touched with a chill. We were both too ridiculous to have thought about packing a lunch or bringing a coat. No one wore hats back then; hats were a style affectation, and their practicality was totally lost on us.

Danny Allen,
watercolor, 1972.
Collection of
Antonio Petracca.

On our way home, the air temperature dropped 30 degrees or more. Thunder and lightning filled the sky while we pedaled our bikes as fast as we could, half to get home and half to keep warm. Big, wet flakes of snow melted on us while we biked like madmen toward the Merriman Street apartment. My bike was older and had fat tires, while Dan was riding a sleek Peugeot he'd borrowed. As we approached the city, Danny called out to me, "Look, no hands!" turning around as he hollered—at which point he rear-ended a parked car and totaled the borrowed Peugeot. It was a thousand-dollar bike, which was a lot of money back then—and still is. We cleaned out our bank account to give the owner checks over several months until it was paid off. The bicycle owner wasn't at all interested in taking some of our artwork to help pay off the debt. Nice try, though.

All Dan would say about that incident—over and over and over—was "I'm an asshole, I'm an asshole." Dan took things to heart far too much, and he berated himself to the point where that foolish bicycle accident was eroding his self-worth. The litany wouldn't stop until he fell asleep. At night, Dan and I would spoon like puppies, even if one of us was crying. Generally speaking, at that point, the one crying was Dan, because he wouldn't let go of the fancy bicycle accident. I, on the other hand, was glad that all he had to show for the disaster was a torn knee on his blue jeans and some scratches. It could have been a lot worse. But Dan often cried, even for no apparent reason, at least no reason he was willing to share. All I could do was comfort him and hope he'd fall back to sleep. I didn't think he was an asshole; I just wished he hadn't busted up the bike. There's a big difference.

Danny Allen, watercolor. Collection of Susan Plunkett.

Right about then, my art career began to gather steam. An article about my Tudor dollhouse ran in the *Rochester Democrat and Chronicle* and was picked up by the *Toronto Globe and Mail,* which expanded on it. I was contacted by the Wagman Gallery in Toronto and asked if I'd be willing to exhibit the dollhouse with them. Of course I agreed. The house had recently returned from the Kodak Gallery in New York, but I'd never thought about it leaving the country—even though Toronto's only a few miles northwest of Rochester. (Years later, after the dollhouse was no longer mine, the poor, de-virginized toy travelled farther; it toured Asia with an exhibit of American crafts.) Dan didn't want to go to Toronto with me, but he made arrangements for his friend David Lortz to drive me there. David was planning to go to Toronto anyway, and his mother was joining us so she could visit a friend who would be in Toronto for a short stay.

The night before launching out for Canada, I had a terrible time sleeping. I kept waking up and having awful fantasies of being stopped at the border and having border agents rip the dollhouse apart, looking for drugs and other contraband. To make matters worse, Natasha was in heat, meowing all over the place. No one slept.

Dan got up, sat at his drawing table with Natasha, and performed a ritual I still find curious. Whenever Natasha went into heat, he'd take a number two sable brush and satisfy her. He did it gently, but Natasha would become passionate as she humped the brush. Dan figured she was horny, so he should let her go at it. I did my best not to dwell on the carryings on in the other room. In my neurotic, paranoid brain, the customs officers were going to tear my dollhouse apart, and all my work would be ruined. I couldn't get the thought out of my head. I heard Dan say, "Chill out," but he wasn't talking to me; he was telling Natasha that her happy-ending massage was over. I'd barely fallen asleep when the alarm awakened me.

Dollhouse-moving day was in early September, in the morning. While I waited for my ride, I kept putting on my coat and taking it off, unable to decide if I was hot or cold. David Lortz and his mother pulled up in front of the house on Merriman Street, and Dan and I began loading David's van with stacks of packed boxes and the dollhouse itself. I'd planned to use nothing but a blanket under the dollhouse for cushioning. I didn't want anything draped over it because any pressure could break off little brackets and details. When Dan and I finished loading the van, he waved goodbye, and off we went.

I sat in back with the dollhouse, doing my best to keep the thing from bouncing around as the van lurched one way or the other. Meanwhile, David's mother henpecked and fishwifed him the whole way to Toronto. She was chiding him for his driving in a tongue-in-cheek way, but she meant every word. David took corners too sharply, and the shock absorbers in his van weren't all that effective.

David's mom was wearing a peacock blue jacket and matching skirt and carrying an old-ladyish purse. As I recall, she was also wearing a hat of a coordinated blue-green, trimmed with netting. David was pretty much silent through the entire trip, with his shoulder-length, dirty-blonde hair blowing out the window and behind the driver's seat toward me. I had my hands full, keeping everything from falling off the house or blowing away in the interior windstorm while keeping the boxes from colliding. Nothing got seriously broken, although some minor repairs ended up being necessary.

Things were going swimmingly until we reached the border between the United States and Canada, when traffic ground to a crawl. Mrs. Lortz launched into David about something mothers launch into, and David took in every word in silence. I had a Charlie horse in one leg and a throbbing backache, and the border patrol was taking its sweet time letting people through. Everybody in one of the cars ahead was asked to get out and open bags and let agents look in the trunk. All the while, cars returning to America were breezing past, slowing down for a moment only to continue speeding their way back to the States.

When our turn for inspection came, the border patrol had David roll down his window. Mrs. Lortz, in a very authoritative voice, leaned over and told the guard, "These two young men are transporting a dollhouse for me." They aimed a flashlight on the dollhouse and me and waved us through. It was as easy as that. Somehow the supposed fact that a middle-aged woman dressed like she was going to church had hired two hippies to move a giant dollhouse didn't look at all odd to the border patrol.

Once we made it to Toronto, we had two stops to make before I was to be dropped off at the gallery. At the first stop, Mrs. Lortz fished something from her purse and something else from the front of her bodice. She handed them to David. He hopped out of the car and gave the parcels to a man who met him by a garage door. David returned with an envelope. Several blocks later, he dropped his mother off at the house where her friend was visiting.

When we were alone in the car, David confessed that he and his mother had just done a dope run but that he hadn't wanted me to know because Danny had told him I was completely uncool. Just as I'd feared for the whole night before our departure, we actually were smuggling dope. The argument between David and his mother had been entirely in code. She hadn't been happy about giving a convincingly innocent cover to his activity because she didn't approve of what he was doing. But the ruse had worked perfectly. Mrs. Lortz had believed that no one would bother a middle-aged lady who looked like she was all dolled up for church, and she was right, at least back in the day.

At last David dropped me off in front of the Wagman Gallery, where assistants helped me carry the dollhouse and boxes inside. David drove off and away. I spent the remainder of the day setting up and furnishing the dollhouse, seeing to it that everything was waxed in place and that all the lights were working. Setting everything up took me well past store hours, and the gallery manager stayed with me while I completed my work. The house was being displayed on a large, antique harvest table that was the first thing you'd see as you passed the gallery from the street. Subtle overhead lighting was aimed at the house so it seemed to glow in the large central window, without bleaching out the effects of the dollhouse's own interior lights.

I attached a custom-cut piece of Plexiglas to the open-ended back so people couldn't reach inside and steal things. The gallery was filled with valuable things—antique Japanese lacquer, carved jade, and priceless antiques, jewelry, and furniture—but none of it really appealed to me, although I appreciated its beauty. The manager made small talk while I worked. When I was done, we went outside and looked at the dollhouse from the street. It was a showstopper. In fact, people were already stopping to look at it. I felt as proud as a champion.

Inside, the manager locked up the front gallery and led me to a back exit through the stockroom. He asked me, "Do you like fine old antiques?" I told him I did. Without missing a beat, the older gentleman undid his pants, took off his belt, and dropped his trousers. It was perfectly clear what I was expected to do—which I did without reciprocation but not without embarrassment. To me, he was ancient, and doing that act to him was disgusting. When the task was completed, he set the alarms, leaving the display lights on to illuminate my dollhouse and other featured items in the gallery.

I left for a youth hostel off Yonge Street, where I shared a bedroom and a bath down the hall for seven dollars a night. On my budget, that was a lot of money. Although it was a shared room, I was the only one there that early in the evening. I finished reading Jane Austen's *Sense and Sensibility* because I'm a dork. Then I got up and walked back to the gallery to take one last look at the dollhouse in the window—right across the street from the prestigious Royal Ontario Museum.

I didn't sleep well for a second night in a row. I don't like sleeping in unfamiliar surroundings. My roommates got in at around three in the morning and talked in French for hours while turning lights on and off. I took the first bus back to Rochester the following morning.

As I sat in the bus, daydreaming and looking out the windows, a strong sense of shame took hold of me. I felt sick to my stomach over having serviced that older man the night before. But I was starting to catch on to how it all worked. Museum and gallery people have a way of using aspiring artists for more than merely their artistic talents. If my work was going to remain on display, I had to pay a price up front.

I'd already had an experience like that when I was a young kid. Looking out the bus window, watching trees and buildings pass, I let myself compare the experiences. Servicing the manager the night before had been perfunctory and joyless, but the time when I was a boy had been more a case of stumbling into an unintentional rite of passage. Neither experience had been truly consensual. I'd been expected to perform in a certain manner, and refusal wasn't an option.

My boyhood introduction to sex developed into a subject of constrained family silence during my early years. No one talked about it, but at least to my mind it was everpresent. I had been exposed to things I wasn't yet ready for, things society wasn't yet ready for. I don't know how old I was, though I've often tried to remember. Was I seven? Or was I nine? The other boy was a high-school teenager who was later sent to reform school. He talked me into following him into a chicken coop by telling me he was hiding a twenty-mule-team Borax model in there, like the one Ronald Reagan advertised on TV during *Death Valley Days*. Once inside the chicken coop, I found no toy stagecoach. We did things I wasn't ready to understand but was fascinated by all the same. And after the older boy—the neighborhood's notorious bad kid—had done what he'd set out to do, he pushed my pants down around my ankles, where they got tangled up with my shoes. He pulled up my shirt so it went around my arms and stuffed some of the striped jersey into my mouth. Then he carried me outside into the bleaching sunlight, like he was showing me off naked, so everyone in the world could see me. I spit the fabric out of my mouth and started to yell and scream

*Danny Allen, watercolor, 1972.
Collection of WTW.*

*Danny Allen, watercolor, 1972.
Collection of WTW.*

*Danny Allen, watercolor, 1972.
Collection of WTW.*

and struggle. To my childish mind, being carried around naked outside was way weirder than the initiation rites that had taken place in the chicken coop.

My teenage molester dropped me and laughed, kicking at me while I rolled around on the ground, working to get my pants back up and my shirt straightened out. I was disgusted by the white discharge he'd left on me, which made my clothes feel sticky and damp. I ran home.

Danny Allen, India ink drawing, 1972.
Collection of WTW.

Having been born plainspoken, I told my mother what had just happened. She was pouring V-8 juice into small, cut-crystal glasses for a Sunday afternoon supper, and she spilled the whole can all over her freshly starched, white-linen tablecloth. My mother was always a master of symbolism. She screamed for my father, and he went down the street and punched out the kid's uncle, who was raising the boy. The police were not to my knowledge called, as this was considered a personal matter. No one had any Sunday supper, and I was kept in my darkened bedroom until the following day—not of my choosing.

The incident was never discussed again. The teenager was no longer in the neighborhood, and my family never mentioned where he'd gone. But I overheard one of the neighborhood kids say he'd been shipped off to a reform school. Someone else said he'd gone to a military academy. I said nothing.

The bus pulled into the Rochester station. I was back home.

By this time in my life, I had more or less lost touch with my parents. Sometimes I called them on holidays or birthdays, if I remembered to do so. But they had to wear me down to get me to give them our phone number. They had my address, and eventually my mother bribed our number out of me by mailing me a check. But the phone was under Dan's name, so they couldn't get it from the telephone operator. My parents didn't know Danny's last name.

One evening the phone rang, and Dan answered it by saying, "This is God speaking."

On the other end was my mother, never to be outdone. She replied, "This is the Virgin Mary. Can you please put my son on the line?"

Dan laughed, but her response had spooked him. My mother has always had that effect on people. She'd be the first to tell you that she was a force to be reckoned with.

Danny Allen, watercolor, not dated.
Collection of Susan Plunkett.

I learned from the call that my parents would be coming to Rochester for a short visit. I don't remember why, but I do recall the way they treated Dan during dinner. They weren't thrilled with my insistence that he be invited at all, but those were my conditions. They made their true feelings known quite clearly nevertheless. In many Italian and Jewish families, people argue and discuss what's on their minds; they even throw things, if necessary. My family members are old WASPs. WASPs never discuss anything meaningful, painful, or uncomfortable. Communication takes place through exasperated facial expressions, loud exhalations, and small talk loaded with sarcasm.

So that's what they dished out to Danny. We went to a steakhouse somewhere in downtown Rochester, and everyone was on edge. My parents were treating Danny like he was my corrupter—hardly the case. I was nobody's virgin. Nor was I what you'd have called a player—certainly not by fast-track gay standards. But my parents treated Dan like he should have been sitting at a different table. I was mortified. Dan got up and left in the middle of the meal, and a beat later I followed, but I couldn't find him.

Every time the phone rang back at the apartment that night, it was my mother, doing everything but apologizing. She could turn any incident into something about herself, and so it went. I met my parents for a haunted and silent breakfast the following morning at their motel before they drove back to their new home in Indianapolis. My father's job had transferred my parents from Moorestown, New Jersey, while I was in college.

By the time I'd returned from breakfast, Dan was at his drawing table. Things were pretty silent there, too. I could tell that he wanted me to leave him alone.

Another family event gave me a chance to know for certain that no one in my family regarded my relationship with Danny as valid. A homosexual love affair, even one that ends with tragedy and death, wasn't quite real to my parents. Had I been married and lost a wife, or even if I'd lost a girlfriend, I would have met with an entirely different set of circumstances, filled with sympathy and caring.

The Christmas after Danny died, I was pressured into taking a flight to Chicago, where my brother and sister-in-law lived. They were basking in the glow of a new baby. Nothing compounds one's personal agony like being surrounded by holiday decorations and the cheerfulness of others. Soon after I arrived, my mother took me aside and said in a stern voice, "I don't want you talking about that boy who died and ruining everyone's Christmas." Just when I needed my parents the most, they insisted I put on an act I was completely incapable of performing.

People have their priorities, and mine was to take every last penny I had and get in a cab that would drive me to the nearest gay bar. I met a nice guy there, who talked to me over the course of a couple of days and let me stay at his apartment. He got me back to my brother's place in time for my family to take me to the airport for my plane ride home.

After that, it took decades for my parents and I to mend our differences. My parents were perpetually looking for answers as to why I was gay, dwelling on things they'd read in *Reader's Digest*. They constructed theories. The fact that my father traveled for business, for instance, had left me with too much mothering and not enough fathering. So my mother took it to be her fault I was gay, which she liked because that made it all about her. This enabled her to put on performances that would have stunned and fascinated Eugene O'Neill.

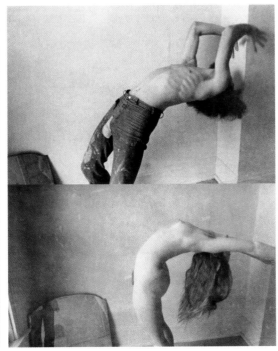

Eva Weiss, diptych photo of Dan and another model.

After Dan was dead, I hardly slept at all. But when I did, I dreamed about him. Sometimes I had my recurring dream about the floating building. Often I dreamed simply of Dan's face, larger in my mind's eye than a whole movie screen. He made familiar facial expressions—smiles, troubled looks, vacant stares.

I would lie awake and think about a huge, non-objective color-field painting that Dan worked on for months. It was beautiful. Then he painted over it all and did another one right on top. The new painting would be every bit as beautiful, only to be primed out again and repainted over and over and over. As poor as we were, surely we could have afforded more canvas. Perhaps Dan was more interested in the process of painting than in the end result. There was an entire one-man show hidden beneath one canvas—concealing layers and layers of lost paintings.

I don't know how it escaped my full understanding, but toward the end of our time together, Dan's behavior became increasingly peculiar with each passing day. I still think about that giant color-field painting in the middle of the night, and the exhibit that could have been.

But there is something more about my years with Dan that still haunts me. I've sat in many a therapist's office and cried over it. I just did so again a couple of weeks back. It's still not easy to talk about, but talk about it I will.

Danny Allen, CASEY AT THE BAT, *unfinished acrylic, ca. 1974. Collection of WTW.*

IT WAS DAN'S RULE that he and I had an open relationship. My ego was caught somewhere between *How is this not like breaking up?* and *How is this possibly going to be comfortable?* I was nestled between Sunday School class and my own inherited attitudes, and there was so much I didn't understand. I held an unspoken belief that sex was the outward physical expression of an inward spiritual love. I wasn't comfortable with bringing other people back to Dan's and my apartment, and to this day I'm not very comfortable having sex at someone else's house. So let's get to the essence: I was not then nor am I now completely comfortable with having sex devoid of love even in the presence of desire. Somewhere along the line, I got the idea in my head that love and sex were connected. But I was coming of age in the late 1960s and early 1970s, which meant that I was living by rules from an outdated manual on sexual etiquette.

So I was supposed to entertain other lovers, but I had an overdecorated, white, minimalist bedroom that was way too foreboding to use. It was a beautiful room to walk into during a snowstorm and then leave to go sit by the radiator, but other than that, it was useless. I have no recollection of ever sleeping through the night in the white bedroom. Dan and I had shared an octagonal bedroom in the turret that was warm and comfortable and that combined our personalities. Our high-backed Victorian bed was floating a bit away from the windows on three of the walls. Then it became Dan's room. But the room also contained my upright piano, which secured me regular entrance.

When I told Dan I didn't understand how to be comfortable in an open relationship and said that it felt all wrong, he gave me a book about Vita Sackville West and Virginia Woolf. I found the book eye opening and clever but felt that it told the story of people living in an alternate universe.

I didn't want to think about the sexual escapades of Virginia Woolf, and the book really didn't help me accept my new role. Was an open relationship like dating while having a steady on the side, or like having a steady while dating on the side? Was it like cheating without guilt, just so long as the encounters didn't mean anything? Which of our activities were we supposed to share, and what should we keep to ourselves? How exactly does a couple go about something like this? I wasn't comfortable with any of it. For his part, Dan kept things simple when it came to outside encounters. I came to understand that they were generally anonymous and took place at a bathhouse, the whereabouts of which remains unknown to me to this day. That was Dan's territory. Not that I'd have found the nerve to go there, but I wasn't supposed to run into him. That went without saying.

Danny Allen. India ink. ca. 1970. Collection of WTW.

Danny Allen. India ink, ca. 1970. Collection of WTW.

I gained my scant personal knowledge of the workings of gay bathhouses in Toronto. A round-trip bus ticket to Toronto was cheap enough, and I was tutored in the tricks by a trick himself, who talked me into going to Toronto with him one weekend, shortly after my first trip with the dollhouse. My primary motivation was to visit the dollhouse on display, which I know is not a normal priority for most people.

The fellow I tricked with was named Tommy. One afternoon, in Rochester, he approached me on the street and asked me to come up to his apartment. Uneasy as I felt, I went through with it. Before I knew what was happening, we were making plans to go to Toronto the very next weekend. It was unclear to me whether this meant I was having an affair or what it signified. Were we supposed to have sex again? Psychosexual guidelines have never come naturally to me. And to put it mildly, for gay men in the 1970s, the new sexual frontier left many men without a map.

Danny Allen, India ink, ca. 1972. ▶
Collection of WTW.

Gay guys came on strong, and you were supposed to exert your newfound openness to gay sexuality. But I didn't have simple baggage where sex was concerned; I had steamer trunks and hatboxes. I did, however, go to Toronto with Tommy that weekend and stayed at a bathhouse he knew about. They had a three-dollar special if you got there on a Friday night before ten and checked out on Sunday before noon. This was a way better deal than the youth hostel. You bought a check-in card at the door so you could come and go as you pleased, and your three bucks bought you a cubicle for the weekend that contained a long, narrow mattress the width of a lawn recliner, along with a locker key that was identical to your door key, which was probably the most deluxe thing about the place.

The idea was to lock up your things and walk around in a dimly lit labyrinth wearing only a skimpy towel around your waist and your keys on a scrunchy around your wrist. Time spent in a bathhouse is a lot like an unfilmed episode of the *Twilight Zone* that never aired because it couldn't make it past the censors. The men seemed very single-minded of purpose, and the most aggressive of them were prone to staring at you with very hungry eyes. Most of the men one encounters in bathhouses are examples of the nocturnal North American lounge lizard—clad only in a towel and a blurred set of boundaries.

Danny Allen, India ink, ca. 1972.
Collection of WTW.

Tommy explained to me how the bathhouse worked. First we walked around in towels and tried to exude an aura of dignity, which comes off as just plain fey-gay when you're a Twinkie in your twenties. We each stuffed a few dollars into the wristband that held our keys and bought a beer at the bar. You're supposed to leave all the coin change in a jar for the jock-strapped bartender because you don't have any pockets. Remember, you're only wearing what's left of your dignity.

The next phase is to sip your beer and look around at all the haunted, hairy old men glaring at you and make sure they understand that you're looking past them and that you're terribly bored, waiting for something better to come along. Next, you down your beer, turn on your heels, storm back to your cubicle, change outfits, and go out to the dance clubs.

The ritual we'd just completed was the first stage of an awkward sort of meet 'n greet in which no one talked to each other. The people were creepy, and the place had awful red lighting, terrible wall-to-wall carpeting, and stained plywood interiors. Of course those were the things that caught my eye. But then again, I avoided looking at everyone else's eyes. Tommy claimed that the baths got much better late at night and into the wee hours of the morning, but I never witnessed one of those better nights or mornings.

Danny Allen, India ink, ca. 1972.
Collection of WTW.

Once we were out on the town, Tommy told me that he hated my shirt and couldn't believe he was being seen with me. I was wearing a long-sleeved green shirt with darker green and white checks on the diagonal. He was embarrassed by my lack of fashion acumen and told me it was mortifying to be out in public with a person wearing something so totally unchic. Personal fashion faux pas aside, we walked around the city and went to the places where you're supposed to be seen—saw what we were supposed to see—and then left, looking fashionably bored. I had to be reminded not to get enthusiastic about a cornice on a building or anything else I saw and liked.

I still wasn't clear as to whether Tommy and I were supposed to do the wild thing again or if this was merely a misguided tour. It turned out to be the latter, which was just as well. He and I lost sight of each other at the Manatee, a legendary, wild gay bar unlike anything to be found in Rochester. Gym bunnies in G-strings were swinging above our heads on seated holsters chained to the ceiling. Disco had just begun to raise its neatly coiffed and sprayed head, and the d.j. was blasting "Rock the Boat, Baby" at seven thousand decibels above the threshold of pain.

I drank my beer and talked to no one—you couldn't hear over the music, anyway. I never quite regained my bearings once I lost track of Tommy, so I found the door and left. I walked alone to the front of the Wagman Gallery to look at my lit-up dollhouse in the window. That end of town isn't deserted, but it wasn't an area that people frequented when they were looking for bars, restaurants, and action. I walked around the city, pretending I knew where I was going, attempting to look bored and to affect the aura of sophistication Tommy had tried to impress upon me. Eventually I returned to the bathhouse, not knowing where else to go.

I showed the bouncer my weekend pass at the door. Next I changed into my towel and keys and did one lap around the interior. I discovered the orgy room and watched for an off-putting moment or two. I was approached by a guy who asked me to join him in the back room, which appeared be a dark, disappearing space tucked behind a black-painted wall, where apparently even more salacious activity was taking place. I declined, panicked, and went back to my cubicle, closing and locking the door behind me. In other words, I hid in my cubicle, unable to be part of what comes naturally to most other male human animals. (If you left your door open, gay zombies took it as an open invitation to enter and molest you.)

Speaking of open, the cubicles didn't have ceilings; they were merely partitions. Annoying red-and-green lights bounced off a mirrored ball up above that kept the ceiling moving with a harsh, synthetic aurora borealis. Loud dance music deafened everyone in the place twenty-four hours a day. I hid in my cubicle feeling like the damned, unable to sleep, read, leave, or participate. I remained alone in my cubicle, trying to find a comfortable way to rest, cover my eyes, and cope with the fact that the bathhouse provided no pillows. All you got was a thin foam mattress with an ill-fitting sheet. A bathhouse is not to be confused with the Ritz.

Thus I put myself through a two-night weekend of isolated madness, pretending for no one's eyes but my own that I was enjoying myself. I did not have sex with anyone, but I did decline several nightmarish offers. I visited some of the Royal Ontario Museum but didn't get to see the whole place. Tommy had disappeared, folding himself into the nooks and crannies of Toronto.

When I got back to Rochester, Dan had a wonderful story to share. I didn't completely believe him, but it was a good story all the same. Dan told me he'd ridden our fat-tired bicycle over to Highland Park, where he saw a naked man running and hiding from tree to tree. The guy turned out to be a priest who put on his "cloth" again after he and Dan had done the deed. As a parting gesture, he offered to hear Dan's confession. On second thought, it was probably true!

I had nothing to report about Toronto. All I did was walk around, suffer through loud music and annoying lighting effects, and occasionally go look at my dollhouse in the gallery window. I felt sleep-deprived for days afterward.

The floor collapsed at the Manatee Bar a few years later, and all the G-stringed go-go boys were stranded on the ceiling, screaming. Before you laugh too hard, consider that people on the dance floor were badly injured. At around the same time, the Toronto bathhouse was raided. All the occupants were frog-marched out onto the street and photographed so their pictures could be published in the newspaper. The police rounded up and took pictures of everyone, from peons to priests and politicians. Fortunately, I was not present for either of those calamities.

All three drawings:
Danny Allen, India ink, ca. 1972.
Collection of WTW.

Danny Allen, watercolor (detail). ca. 1972.
Collection of WTW.

What I miss most about Rochester is the generosity of the characters who populated that neurotic little city. Those people were my saving grace. Rochester had perfected its own salon society, a thing that existed nowhere else I'd been. As I noted earlier, this unique cultural habit had probably been born of the cabin fever induced by generation after generation of winter blizzards. People entertained in Rochester. I heard the word "brunch" for the first time while living there, because my friend Josef and his partner Richard threw chic Sunday brunches, at which our friend Adele provided hilarious improvisational entertainment. We never heard the noise of a television set broadcasting sporting events in the background, but instead enjoyed stylish conversation and good humor with a background of Cole Porter tunes, lightly performed by Ella Fitzgerald on albums played on a fancy stereo.

The food was always delicious and inventive, and sometimes it bore exotic foreign names. I'm bad at remembering menu details but good at eating what's put in front of me. Before food was served, heavy, colorful books might be passed around while people conversed—books with photos of English gardens or classical art and architecture. Whether the event was a brunch or a dinner, certain key players would be present wherever you were, ready to pick up where they'd left off on collective gossip and conversations.

The hippie crowd started to grow up, get jobs, move away, or change, which is what comes of all youthful trends. But there were still earth-mother suppers at Diana the Witch's apartment, where the music could be anything from Yma Sumac to Joni Mitchell as Diana dominated the conversation with her surreal non sequiturs. She entertained a less structured flow of guests, who would arrive and leave by their own mysterious schedules. Or sometimes Dan and I were invited to an event by the newly emerging gay boys who were just starting to get gym-toned physiques and short, shagged haircuts. Those mustachioed young men could put together a pretentious dinner party like nobody's business. It was expected that guests were never to be seen in the same outfit twice, which for me was and remains a financial burden that I choose not to meet. People came and went, playing records that showcased the new dance music—most of which was not as cerebral or introspective as hippie folk and rock had been. A new era was dawning.

The Memorial Art Gallery curators also threw stylish, well-attended dinner parties, where the food was glorious and made from recipes found in *Mastering the Art of French Cooking*, which was something people other than me seemed to know about. Generally, dinner conversations started out erudite and raced downhill with every glass of wine, reaching the most hilarious, lowest common denominator by evening's end. I still covet the fruit compote in the middle of the curator's dining table, which was topped by a good-sized neoclassic bronze male nude wearing a detachable fig leaf. Once the fig leaf was removed, dinner was served up, along with delicious dishes of gossip, interspersed with high-toned observations about art, then shifting back to discussions of humanity's more basic instincts and bodily functions. Even the furniture blushed.

There were always invitations for two pocket-poor artists, Danny and me. Yet for all the fun and banter at those parties, there was a quiet undercurrent at play for the two of us. Whereas I was uncomfortable in bars and bathhouses, Dan was uncomfortable in the more chic social environments, often withdrawing inside himself and barely contributing to the conversation. Occasionally he'd even draw on his napkin, providing it wasn't linen. We were still viewed as a couple, but we were morphing apart, like plants of a similar appearance that thrive in entirely different types of soil.

About a month or two after I'd brought the dollhouse to Toronto, I got a call from the Wagman Gallery. The dollhouse would no longer light up, and they'd unplugged it due to an odor that suggested an electrical problem. The lights were supposed to be on a timer, but the timer had failed and burned out the transformer. They asked me to come up to repair the electrical system, since the dollhouse was scheduled to be on display through the Christmas holidays and into early January.

Danny Allen, self-portrait,
India ink, undated,
Xerox copy from his missing journals.

Dan had gotten moody—or should I say moodier? I told him I was going to have to go to Toronto to swap out the transformer in the dollhouse and repair the lighting, and I invited him to go with me. I wasn't sure how we'd work the accommodations, given our miniscule earnings, but he was quick to decline anyway. He said he wanted his space and some time alone.

I bought tiny light bulbs, electrical tape, wire, and a new, heavy-duty transformer. The Wagman Gallery was going to provide a better timer device that would control how many hours the house was lighted. I was set to leave that Saturday in the late morning and to return on either Sunday or Monday, depending on how long the repairs took me.

Halloween fell on a Thursday that year, but everyone we knew was celebrating the holiday on Friday night. By this time in Rochester's history, the town had its own gay dance bar called Jim's—which was allegedly a step up from the depressing, dark little hole called Dick's 43, which had been the only gay bar in town, or at least the only one I knew about. You really didn't want to be seen coming or going from Dick's 43 Lounge. It either actually had a dirt floor or simply appeared to, and customers were pie-eyed by noon—men weeping, with mascara running down their cheeks. In contrast, Jim's had a disc jockey, mirrored walls, flashing lights, and a spinning disco ball. It wasn't Studio 54, but at least the owners were attempting to enter the disco era, a beat late.

Jim's also had a dance floor and strobe lighting. And it was where Danny and I planned to celebrate Halloween.

We didn't dress up much that year; instead, we wore black and white masks. Dan chose the black mask, and I wore the white. We closed the club that night, laughing, dancing, and drinking house vodka mixed with orange juice. One previous Halloween, Dan had made a name for himself by wearing a burnt orange, panne velvet evening gown with high heels, a ladies' bathing cap, and a dead bat hanging on a string around his neck. Fortunately the bat wasn't carrying anything contagious. But during our Halloween dance-a-thon, we wore costumes that revealed us as ourselves: gay boys in T-shirts and blue jeans. We lost the masks early in the evening. Danny took me by surprise and kissed me while we were still in the middle of the dance floor. Let the world look; I loved it.

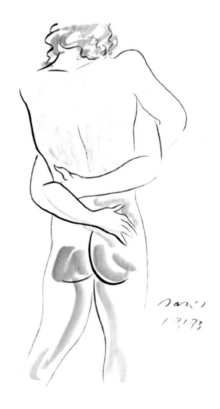

Danny Allen. EMBRACE. *India ink and watercolor. 1973. Collection of WTW.*

Danny Allen,
India ink and
watercolor, 1972.
Collection of WTW.

Danny Allen, India ink, ca. 1973.
Collection of WTW.

Danny Allen, India ink,
ca.1970.
Collection of WTW.

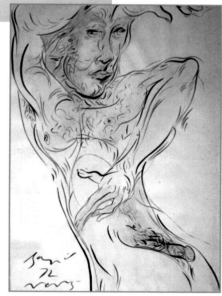

In spite of our alcohol intake, we had enough energy to make love when we got home, but I was a train wreck by Saturday morning. I was glad I'd packed and pulled everything together the day before. When I left to catch the bus in the morning, Dan was so groggy that he wasn't fully awake when I kissed him good-bye, but I remember his smell. Dan had his own special aroma. It was familiar to me, like I'd known it long before I'd met him. He smelled like love to me. He had a scent to his scalp, and I'd bury my nose there when we cuddled. That morning, as I kissed him goodbye, he pulled a pillow over his head and turned over to go back to sleep. I left.

I got into Toronto much later than I'd hoped. The bus had gotten stuck behind an accident for what seemed like hours. Saturday was a far less productive day than I'd planned on, and evening hours at the gallery weren't available. In any case, I didn't want to put in any more evening hours at that gallery.

As I walked around Toronto, trying to look like I had a purpose, I tried to imagine what it would be like to live in that sophisticated city. I was just another face in the crowd, and I could do anything I wanted, but I didn't know what I wanted to do. I went into stores where I couldn't afford anything, ate as cheaply as I could, and checked back into the Toronto bathhouse to use it like Hell-House Hotel. On Halloween weekend, it almost was the Hell-House Hotel. Men walked around naked or half-naked, wearing Halloween devil masks or anything outrageous, which accentuated their nudity. And not revealing their faces seemed to make the patrons even more brazen.

I needed to use the bathhouse as a home base, but what was going on inside did nothing to entice me. I was scared to death of the place. The atmosphere didn't beckon me; I had no urge to throw myself feet first into the orgy room, nor to display myself with my towel artfully draped and the door left open, as many of the men did. I have a special talent for figuring out how to be com-pletely out of place almost anywhere I go.

However, the bathhouse did have a phone booth, which was a quaint modern convenience at the time. Lonely, I placed a call home to Dan. He sounded high. He also sounded depressed and incoherent. Dan was on something. I was used to that, but from so far away, I had no idea what he was on. Intense weed? Some kind of pill? He wasn't making sense. I knew he was taking antidepressants,

Danny Allen, Splitting Migraine,
sepia ink, ca. 1972. Collection of WTW.

Danny Allen,
India ink, 1972.
Collection of WTW.

Danny Allen,
India ink, 1972.
Collection of WTW.

but he was also taking or drinking whatever was made available to him. I tried to find out what was going on, but he cut me short, saying he needed to go.

I made that phone call on Sunday, after relighting and repairing the dollhouse. I planned to return home the following day, after taking in the Royal Ontario Museum, which I hadn't investigated to my satisfaction. But I still had one more night to pass in the bathhouse.

There is no way of determining whether it's night or day when you're in a bathhouse. Natural light is on the other side of the rock you're under. But I knew it was night, and I knew that sleep would be elusive. So I hid in my cubicle and was ticking away the time when a knock came at my door. I opened the door just a peek, assuming it was the management telling me that if I wasn't fucking or running around naked, then I wasn't supposed to be there.

But I was wrong. A gay bathhouse is an upscale version of what I imagine a flophouse to be like, with vinyl mattresses and the vague aroma of bug spray. I opened the door and saw a balding, young blonde man with a scraggly beard. He was dressed in the customary shorty towel and wrist key-band. He told me he'd been watching me come and go and wondered why I never left my cubicle. I felt compelled to tell him to take a good look around him for a solid answer to that question, but I refrained.

His name was Len or Lenny. He asked me to dress in a towel and get my keys, because he was going to buy me a drink. I was bored, so I agreed. My brain ached from the incessant loud music and the flashing lights, and I could barely hear myself accepting his invitation because someone had cranked up the sound system even louder. They were playing "Rock the Boat, Baby" again. I closed the door to change into my towel and keys. Modesty is among the rarest of qualities in a bathhouse.

Lenny and I ordered beers. The bar light offered just enough illumination for me to tell that he was probably younger than me but that he looked older because of his beard and thinning hair. I don't remember much of what we talked about. I did recall Tommy's advice: to appear disinterested at all times and to give off the aura of being above it all. The advice was coming naturally to me, working beautifully with my insecurities and dovetailing with my deep distrust of the bathhouse environment.

Danny Allen, watercolor, 1972. Collection of WTW.

Danny Allen.
India ink, 1972.
Collection of WTW.

The towels weren't nearly as large as real towels. They required constant re-tucking, even though I probably only had a thirty-inch waist at the time. Lenny's junk was falling out below his towel, and he was defying me not to look at it. The sight of him wasn't making me think wild thoughts or devise a plan to jump his bones. He was nice enough, bland, not bad looking or good looking, just average. As the gay boys say, "Good from far, far from good." I decided this wasn't really going to go anywhere, thanked him for the drink, excused myself, and went back to my cubicle.

A little while later, another knock came at my door. It was Lenny again. He asked if I'd open the door so he could ask me a question—so I did. He asked me what was wrong with him and what I didn't like about him. He started to cry. He told me that everyone had turned him down or ignored him. He was sobbing.

He sat on my cot and told me that no one ever noticed him. He told me that he'd looked old before he'd ever gotten a chance to feel young. Suddenly I found myself comforting an imperfect stranger on a vinyl-covered foam cot in a Toronto bathhouse. I told Lenny that he wasn't terrible; it was the place that was terrible. Instinctively, I put my arms around him and rocked him while

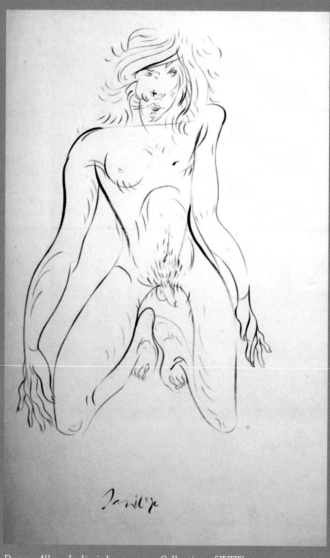

Danny Allen, India ink. ca. 1970. Collection of WTW.

he cried. I'd held Dan that very same way countless times. Before long, I was kissing Lenny, and soon we were engaged in what can only be categorized as a mercy fuck.

And this pitiful event happened to coincide with what must have been a period of desperately brutal pain in the life of the only man I'd ever loved and ever would love. I was pitching a mercy-fuck to a person I knew nothing about while my own lover was in indescribable emotional desperation—so much so that he had led himself to the Driving Park Bridge to throw his body to its death. But I didn't know that yet.

Danny Allen,
graphite, 1973.
Collection of WTW,
gift from John Grace
and Nelson Baldo.

I let Lenny out of my lair and had a nauseating sensation of vertigo. A piercing thrill went through the pit of my chest. I felt like I was peeking over the edge of the observation deck on top of the Empire State Building. I felt the free-fall of a roller coaster and had an intense desire to be safe at home—to be anywhere but where I was.

I spent another hellish night lying awake in that bathhouse, feeling like throwing up. I've never been to one of those places since, except to drop off safe-sex AIDS pamphlets I designed, but that's a whole other veil of tears.

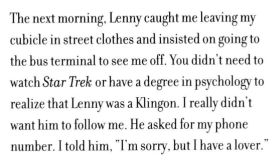
Danny Allen, ballpoint pen, ca. 1974. Collection of WTW.

The next morning, Lenny caught me leaving my cubicle in street clothes and insisted on going to the bus terminal to see me off. You didn't need to watch *Star Trek* or have a degree in psychology to realize that Lenny was a Klingon. I really didn't want him to follow me. He asked for my phone number. I told him, "I'm sorry, but I have a lover."

I can't usually read for long on moving buses, trains, or airplanes. What I can do is look out windows and fall into my own thoughts. And on that ride home, I felt ill. Life almost never surprises me, but it does shock me. I felt a foreboding as I looked out at the landscape passing by.

At last I arrived home and walked into Dan's and my apartment to find it full of people. There was no music. Everyone looked somber. I don't recall if it was twilight or merely a dark day, but everything seemed dim. I don't remember who told me that Danny was dead and how he had died, but I went numb. I let out sounds that seemed to come from somebody else, but I knew they were my own. News that devastating sinks in in waves, in jolts, in tremors, in tears and abject emptiness. To protect yourself, you allow your mind to indulge in a fruitless longing to roll back the calendar to simpler times that will never, ever be again.

Danny Allen, India ink, 1972. Collection of WTW.

Stories about Danny's suicidal tendencies have come my way since that day. In around 1967, several years before I met Danny, he'd taken a drafting class with a fellow named Bruce, who years later became a part of the same brunch and dinner-party circuit as Dan and me. Bruce told me that Dan had been light years ahead of the rest of the drafting class and could probably have taught a thing or two to the instructor. Bruce and Danny became fast friends and hung out in a circle of other artists and creative people, all of whom decided one day to have an elegant picnic in Letchworth State Park. They thought it would be fun to shock the visiting suburban families by dressing their picnic table with a damask tablecloth, fine china, silver utensils, and stemware for their wine. So this motley collection of hippies sat down to a late-afternoon, candlelit table fit for a king, surrounded by majestic, craggy mountains and bluffs. Away from prying eyes, they smoked a joint in the woods and washed it back with wine, which seemingly enhanced the beauty and mystery of the wilderness setting.

After the meal was over, Danny started to climb up the rocks, going higher and higher. Bruce and his friends on the ground called after him, pleading with him to come back down to earth, because the places he was climbing toward had started to frighten everyone. But the more they protested for him to return to safer ground, the higher and more defiantly Dan climbed until he reached the uppermost perch, even as rocks crumbled beneath his footfalls. Once he'd reached the apex of his upward journey, Danny posed like a crucifix, poised as if ready to launch into a swan dive. This sent shock waves through all who witnessed it. Having achieved his goal and ultimate effect, Dan climbed back down, to the relief of his entire party and the others who'd gathered to watch, spellbound with anxiety. When Bruce learned that Danny had taken his own life and how he had done so, this recollection sent cold shivers through him.

I have been told there was a sole pedestrian on the footpath of the Driving Park Bridge that day in November, a pedestrian who saw a man run past at full speed and jump the guardrail of the bridge. He did it the way anyone would jump a garden gate or do a hurdle in a track event. He leaped over the side of the bridge without hesitation or pause. This witness notified the police. Hardened officers on the beat call a person who jumps off a bridge a *jumper*. The word sends a chill through me.

I can still close my eyes and see Danny's face, whether quizzical, comical, or deep in thought, while he drew on a Marlboro or a joint, bit his fingernails to the quick, or did all three things at once. I can hear in my mind the cadence of his voice. But I can't distinguish his words. Why can I remember so few of his words? I remember very little of what he said to me, but I recall vividly almost everything he taught me. He taught me how to paint, how to look at things and really see them, as if for the first time. He taught me to love and to make love, and then he took it away—or perhaps I never learned how to let go, or how to let the loss be and to become whoever I am on my own. I never learned how to be with people, any more than I learned how to be alone, but I've made peace with being by myself.

In the daze I entered after his death, I allowed my friends to make all my decisions, all except the laying out of clothes for Dan's body. I chose the red-and-yellow platform shoes and the shirt he'd worn the last night we'd danced together. After that, I was cut loose. The people in my circle didn't feel it was appropriate for me, the gay lover, to attend a Catholic funeral service. I seem to recall Diana the Witch having something to do with that decision. So I was sent to New York to stay with my friend Frank until Dan's funeral was over. I was told that the church was packed to capacity. Dan was a well-loved person; people loved his creativity, his quirkiness, and his Pan-like countenance. Few of them had known the depths of his troubles.

Years later, Nancy Rosin told me about the day of Dan's death and the funeral that ensued. Nancy also recalled seeing schools of bats in the sky the last time she saw Dan, the night before he died. At the time of his death, Nancy was living with her partner, Christine, who worked for the Rochester *Democrat and Chronicle*. Unbeknownst to me, a reporter from that newspaper also lived in the Merriman Street house where Dan and I shared the top floor. He heard over the wire that a

*Danny Allen, graphite.
Collection of Gary Clinton.*

Danny Allen, 1971, in Diana's living room.

young man with his address had jumped off the Driving Park Bridge. Christine told Nancy, and immediately they thought that it had to have been Danny.

Earlier that day, Eva Weiss had called Nancy to see if she knew where Dan was. Eva had gotten an uneasy feeling after talking to him, probably at around the same time as I'd called him from the bathhouse. Nancy, Christine, and Eva were already overcome with foreboding by the time the name of the body was confirmed. Word spread through Rochester like wildfire.

Nancy wrote the following passage to me decades after the fact:

> I think it's tempting to look back on our lives then as irresponsible or out of touch. But I never have. I feel like we were deeply in touch. But we were so young then, kind of in various stages of pre-therapy. There was something exhilarating about completely acting out our jumbled inner lives.

At one point, Nancy asked her therapist if she would ever feel so passionately about life again, once she understood herself, and she got no solid answer.

Nancy recalled,

> *Living almost on thin air, we kept a job just to buy the time needed to make art. Or loving someone with all your heart, not realizing that all this could come to an end. For me, Danny's death was that awakening.*

Dan's death was an awakening for us all, splintering a core group of friends, who sought lives in different cities or stayed in Rochester but approached life differently from that day forward. A band of free spirits felt suddenly grounded, grounded in ways both healthy and sad. The world became far too real. All of our fanciful dreams about making art and being totally free were abruptly replaced with the slap of discovering how fragile and fleeting our time on this earth really is.

Nancy had loved Danny like a brother. They'd often taken freelance work together, painting houses while talking about life and love. Her powerful words reverberated through me:

> *I don't romanticize Danny's mental illness. Jumping off a bridge speaks volumes about the pain, anguish, and anger that he suffered. I've often imagined that all he felt when he took that final step was just relief.*

Years after Dan's death, Nancy ran into Diana the Witch after Diana had received extensive therapy and medication through a psychiatrist. Diana had become a completely different person. She spoke in a monotone, with no affect. She told Nancy that she hated her medication, as she could no longer dream. Is this what would have happened to Dan, if he'd been treated for his mental illness? So much of Dan's art was shaped by that illness.

Eva, Nancy, and I have shared the same ponderings: What would Dan have been like, had he lived? If he was treated for his mental illness, would he have ceased to have that spark that defined him? Would he have been one of the early casualties of the AIDS epidemic, or would time and maturity have led him to make more mature choices? Dan would be sixty-six years old, were he alive today. But in our collective memories, he will always be an impish, Pan-like faun, captivating everyone he touched, creating mysterious artworks, living his secrets, and forever espousing an unexpected turn of phrase.

When I returned from New York after the funeral, I floated around Rochester for a few years. My family was no longer living in New Jersey, and I couldn't picture myself moving to live with them in Indianapolis. I didn't know where else to go, so I stayed put.

I slept in Diana's basement for a while. I slept on the very same cot where Dan had once stayed. Diana took things from me back then. She stole things Dan had made, drawn, or written. I can only assume they're gone now, given Diana's health and mental condition. I got an apartment on University Avenue shortly after Dan died, though I don't have a clue how I got there or who moved me. I was asked to leave because I ran Dremel drills and tools while building my miniature furniture, which fucked up everybody's television reception. Television always wins.

After that, I stayed with a boyfriend at an insane interior decorator's place near the Susan B. Anthony house on Madison Street. That boyfriend left me for another guy he met on a family vacation, leaving me stuck with an apartment I couldn't afford, so I had to give it up. The decorator/landlord let me store all my stuff in the garage. I rode my bicycle around for several days, not letting anyone know I didn't have anywhere to go. Anything was preferable to Diana's basement.

Then I crashed at my friend John's house for a while, got stoned a lot, and carved some of the missing life-sized Victorian appointments for the cornice of the house he was restoring, in trade for an efficiency apartment. Once I took an overdose of pills, not knowing that taking every pill you could get your hands on wasn't necessarily going to kill you. I took enough pills to knock myself out for a couple of days, leaving me to wake up in my own urine. I remember Diana taking me to the hospital after John opened up the apartment because no one had seen me for a while. I remember the sunlight bleaching my eyesight. I discharged myself from the hospital by walking out the door, without anyone stopping me, without signing any legal papers. I lived in a perpetual disjointed fog.

Eventually I was handed the live-in-caretaker position at the Campbell Whittelsey House museum, back in the Cornhill District. I still had Danny's cat, Natasha, and a stray red dog I'd named Autumn. I gave tours of the house museum. Some days I hung shows at the Rochester Memorial Art Gallery, including the Finger Lakes Exhibit, which led to my posthumously submitting Danny's little painting *Sunny Ducks* and to its inclusion in the show.

With permission from Danny's parents, I re-submitted *Sunny Ducks* after the show came down to be considered for the permanent collection. The painting was accepted as a gift in Dan's memory. I'm told it hung for a while in the office of a subsequent museum director, long after I relocated to Philadelphia.

But I haven't the slightest idea where many of Dan's artworks have landed. After his death, I gave most of his art away to our friends, believing at the time that spreading his art out into the world ensured a larger prospect for its survival, and for the most part, I was right. However, one building where some of his wonderful, whimsical circus drawings hung burned to the ground, taking those delicate little pieces with it. Life and luck can be as random as strikes of lightning.

Life threw me another curveball when I started to lose my eyesight quickly due to detached retinas. Things I looked at became wavy. I was and am to this day haunted by colored lights, worse than you'd see in a disco or a bathhouse, which often obscure my vision. I had retinal surgery at Rochester's Strong Memorial Hospital, which left me with central vision only in my left eye and damaged periphery in both. I was in the hospital with sandbags on either side of my head, being told not to move, not even to go to the bathroom, only to lie perfectly still, in a total panic—until further notice.

Rod Serling of *Twilight Zone* fame died on the other side of the wall while I was having my surgery performed. I only had detached retinas, but the brilliant Mr. Serling died during open-heart surgery, following what had been thought to be a minor heart attack. In the episode "A Game of Pool," written by George Clayton Johnson and aired on October 31, 1961, a character says something that applies here:

As long as they talk about you, you're not really dead. As long as
they speak your name, you continue. A legend doesn't die, just
because the man dies.

I'm certain that Mr. Serling passed an earwig through the wall that's been
nibbling away at my sanity ever since.

While alone in the Campbell Whittelsey House, recovering from surgery,
I had a nervous breakdown—or perhaps *meltdown* is a better word. Every
nerve ending in my body jittered with panic and fear. Animals can be so
remarkable; at night, Natasha Sweetmeat crawled on top of me to purr and
knead my chest. Autumn lay beside me and nestled her snout into the nape
of my neck, and the two of them finally lulled me to sleep. But in daylight, my
blind panic would return with the light, which hurt my eyes. I bloodied all my
fingernails down to the quick, and I trembled with raw fear.

Eventually I stopped showing up at the Memorial Art Gallery and was replaced.
I stopped going out to the Strong Museum, too, but the employee turnover was
so bizarre that I'm not sure anyone ever noticed.

I needed my life to change, but I wasn't sure how to make this come about.
I began by redistributing my earthly load. I gave Danny's cat, Natasha, to his
mother because it seemed like the right thing to do. I gave my dog, Autumn,
to a young couple who could give her a far better home than I could. I sold the
Tudor dollhouse to a known collector for next to nothing. She sold my dollhouse to an important museum in Kansas City for thousands and thousands
more than I'd been paid. I lost most of the little money I'd made on the dollhouse by investing it in Kodak stock that I was advised to buy; I was told it was
about to split. Instead, Kodak was sued by Polaroid for industrial espionage
and later was broken up by the government's antitrust laws. I was merely another of the many little people harmed and ripped off by the greedy bungling
of powerful people.

While still in emotional limbo, I became friendly with a lesbian named Leslie.
She told me I was an ass for not picking up the broken pieces of my life and
moving on. Leslie would tear the filters off a couple of Marlboros, light them
both at once, hand me one, and tell me to smoke it like it was a Lucky Strike or
a joint. She told me to be a man and start again. She told me to bring structure

Danny Allen, watercolor, ca. 1972.
Collection of WTW.

to my life and take advantage of the talent and gifts I'd been given. Leslie made a profound mark on me and then, without warning, she simply wasn't around anymore. I ran into a mutual friend, who said, "Oh God, Bill. Didn't you hear? Some drunk driver crossed lanes, and Leslie was killed instantly. The funeral was two weeks ago." Another person lost; another funeral I had missed. I had to get the hell out of Rochester, New York, and all its pretty Victorian houses, seven-foot snowdrifts, and more toxic memories waiting for me around every corner than any person should be asked to endure.

I bought an interview suit. A wonderful musician-friend drove me down to Philadelphia, along with my clothes, a table, a chair, a lamp, and a mattress. And, of course, Danny Allen's portfolio, containing all the pieces that were left after I'd distributed art to the people who loved him.

I built a whole new life in Philadelphia. I experienced love again, though never with the same intensity. I had losses, too, but I have survival skills that no one but me can ever understand. I came to Philadelphia to live my day-to-day challenges, just like everyone else. But that is an entirely different story.

I sat in my lawyer's office better than a year ago, reading the first draft he'd prepared of my will. After both of your parents are gone, you think about practical, mortal things like that. At least I did, after the collective mess my parents had made of their wills.

"Am I correct in reading," my lawyer said, "that your Pompeian bronze penis-shaped door handle goes to your friend Kevin, should you predecease him?"

"Yes," I replied.

"I've never heard those words used together in the same sentence," he said. "The table you designed and had built, you want the woodworker's daughter to have it. Do you have her contact information?"

"I can get it," I said.

"And I have a note here that says you want Danny Allen's portfolios to be left to his family, once you have located his relatives. Oh, and there's one last thing," my lawyer said without looking up. "What do you want done with your ashes?"

I was sitting in the lawyer's office, looking out of a high-rise window at a sky in motion, daydreaming like I was on a bus to nowhere. I thought for a moment and replied, "I want them scattered from the Driving Park Bridge in Rochester, New York." Better late than never.

Danny Allen, unfinished miniature painting, acrylic on board,
3 ½ x 3 inches, ca. 1974.
Collection of WTW.

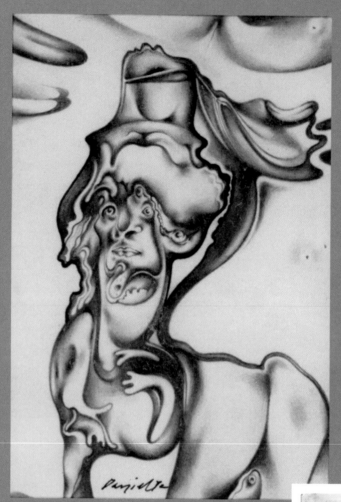

Danny Allen, graphite, ca. 1974.
Gift to WTW from R. James Cromwell.

Here you see the same image before and
after aging and removal of a glued-on mat.
The larger image shows how the art initially
appeared, the smaller image below shows
the piece as it aged.

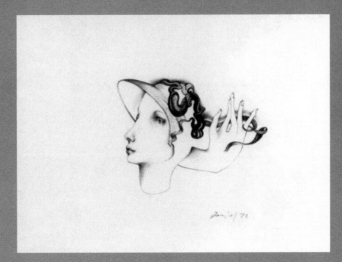

Danny Allen, graphite, 1972. Collection of R. James Cromwell.

Danny Allen, graphite, 1972. Collection of Wendy Lippman.

Danny Allen,
tiny graphite with highlighting, 1972.
Collection of Wendy Lippman.

A POETIC ADDENDUM OF WRITINGS
BY DANIEL ARTHUR ALLEN

Danny Allen wrote the following poems over the course of several years toward the end of his life. I believe the writings were in progress at the time I met him, and polished and changed during the years we lived together in the early 1970s. I found several stanzas typed out, but most of it was written in Dan's own hand. He numbered the stanzas, some of which are missing.

Dan gave Eva Weiss a photocopy to read, and she saved it all these years. Diana Wilber took the original folio, which contained all of Danny's journals, out of my things while I was staying with her. Diana is now in a nursing home, and the originals are assumed to be lost.

I can never thank Eva enough for her love and support, and for the invaluable assistance she lent by helping me transcribe Dan's words.

Danny Allen, collage, not dated. Collection of WTW.

CHAPTER ONE

ANXIETY #1

Tonight I have a new pad of paper to write on but I feel
disconcerted having a light shine behind me. I feel more
comfortable with the sun at my front than my back, as if
someone were watching. But the someone is only a light
stand shining . . . still I won't move to turn it off. I feel safety
in this uncomfortably wonderful circumstance. Look at me!
Study carefully the acne pits you will find. And upon inspection you'll see my eyes burning into your mind until you feel
the command to turn away. "Do not look now, but know the
presence is real and forever."

*Danny Allen, journal page,
saved by Eva Weiss.*

#2 DEATH

Maturing is like frying, as damp is to drying on a doorway to
death. It is closer with each word that I write and you read.
Ticking. The time is fleshing away used cells, replacing them
with ones which may be stronger but not last longer.

#3 TIME

Mama warns them: "My children watch the birdie. Smile."
Cheese is mild, or, is it strong? "When you smile, hide,
sing this song: Way up on high the downy mane, sing,
string along. The beads of time go marching on the lady's
boarding house."

#4

The trip to penitence, the zoo of quantum. Psycho tripping
in grey overt tonalities of very similar studies. Fugues by
Bach and sonnets by Shakespeare are meaningful in limited
variable ways. Today's picture is not of an abstract cow, but
of unreal pretended realities. If you can touch, see, feel or
smell it…well, does that make anything real?

#5 TIME

You know you exist in a permanent state of impermanency.
And you know that nothing you may do will save you from
mortality. Still, you hope to be remembered forever, but not
the unremembered one.

#6

The stars shine brightly, though you cannot see them
through the fog. But they are there in the sky shining. Are
you sure? Yes, I saw them yesterday. What did they look
like? I don't know. I could not see them through the fog.

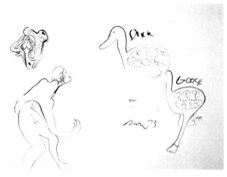

Danny Allen, India ink, ca. 1973.
Collection of WTW.

#7
Only hen scratches result in edible eggs. All are ovular.

#8 TIME
When you're measuring inches use miles for the meters
crows for the rabbits and Jim's for the burghs. Happenstance edges on boundaries abound, amusement as lovers
of flesh people stew in the years of the inches measured by
ants.

#9 MOVING FROM PLACE TO PLACE
Without a suitcase to travel I skirt basic mines of hemlines
with dirt. (Missing mistletoe and tragedies of united hate.)
You think balance is needed for wholeness? Anything ap-
pears unbalanced when compared to something unlike itself.
Then balance happens.

#10 WATER
He comes from the water with stirrings of blasphemy and
conscience: a water baby of large sizes dry to the touch,
inside my plexus winning my love. I'm getting to know him
but he won't tell me the secrets of invisibility.

#11
If you are an alcoholic, I'll drink to that on ice.

#12

Hello red booklet, eyelets and whiplashes. Iris and her pupils think madly and a blank line goes forth from the center of her nose. Gotcha my gosha galoshes, rubbers and ruby tube tooties. January frosts the pain of December's losses. February sounded and looked much better at eight than at twenty-six. There was cold ice and I skated the world away last winter I was eight again. I wore small ice skates and received purple toenails until June grew them away forever.

#13

Counting bacteria is high when the existence of germs is a lie. If violets grow on a hillside of snow and daffodils bloom in the Seine? In the Seine, in the spring, it's all the same thing. Dices are loaded for seven. The alternative of speaking of Heaven is speaking to hell. A lie knows what a hole is by the size of her tongue on the rim. Ram her in. She said Warsaw was raw, but she had no idea how rare.

#14

A hurricane of rejection: vampirish toothless licking and sticking stamps for the Queen of the Bees. (To send out some letters in postcards of pretense.) The mailman knocks wood, his vagina is bleeding, and Iris is close to his breeze. She would know how to fraction

a second if asked. A grimace of pleasure would streak cross her brow roaming with wrinkles and buffalo cows. Her mailbox is foaming with loathing and her pelvis is winding willow trees around.

#15 GOLDEN NAILS
This is my life at age twenty-five in 1972: making lumber advertisements, five columns by ten inches. Smoking cigarettes, chewing my fingernails and putting common things in everyday arrangements. Golden nails are a reoccurring passion. I should grow more on these fingers, but really don't want to.

CHAPTER TWO

#16 WATER
The gurgles float downstream in a jellybean. I see a young woman float on the sea. "A donut for you." She passes and dies and makes waves for the warmth in the froth of her mouth.

#17
There are bones for the masses, a delight for the king who amasses from sugar on a licorice string. Melting to syrups the crystals dare dry, becoming tanned jewels on calcified hide. Reams of darkness lay between these three bright strata's of light. They divide the day into patterns of equal divisions of light. The King attempts to be what he's not: a victor of spoils whose ribbons he ties into images of unending truth—fearing his. Is not this a mode made by our souls? It's an art for glass fingers only; pounding rocks at the side of a stream, cutting paper rainbows with watery shears, and killing consciousness with nails of gold.

CHAPTER THREE

#18

A tower of power grows true without leaves. It goes and it comes and it leaves. It prunes the branches. It sorts them to list the time that it takes the limbs and the roots to become the planted design.

#19

I couldn't find you though I wasn't really looking. I wouldn't find you for I was looking in all the wrong places purposely. Who would I have to thank if you found me? You are searching in all the places I am not. Why do we play this dangerous game, with all the uncertainty of pretended safety?

#20

I'm looking through pages and pages of my mutilated memory, attempting to find a settling down print, and finding a settling down print in the dark side of the moon.

#21

A knot is not a knot; a not is knot a not.

#22

Breakfast of champions: I dream of you. Actually I rarely dream of muscled hunks of male meat. I daydream for these creatures. Those hairy heaving darkly crested chesty shadows drip on down as I lick passionately the grooves of his imaginary younger years. Some think licking a refriger-

ator's asshole is more satisfying, but not to the refrigerator. So lick something on someone who will appreciate it. He will never think of you or thank you, though be consoled: he will love it.

#23
Drop yourselves along the line of Crete and remain yourselves: a mashed Christ on the mast of Christ.

#24 BLUE PLACES
High-heeled hussy with a cock, with balls you stop up to the gangplank. You call for the cops, "come get me." And when the penny anti bed wetter comes, you'll be waiting for her dirty high heel sneakers to ream you. And you'll play the hotsie-totsie blues for the blue bum-buster.

CHAPTER FOUR

#25
"It's a round in a ball on a wall in the hall. It's a square in a cube like some ice it's a nice." This is the story Uncle Ben tells us when he's not here. He could find like as in as, as in ass, as in hole, as in asinine, as in when will he end his story? It made more sense before her began telling it. Uncle Ben is adrift in a sea of brown rice. It is nice.

#26 BLUE PLACES
We wish you a Merry Christmas, darling. When did you find the key to our tombs I am blue chambers? You are nautilus nightly. You send us out and in again. We two are not blue. Our circles complete. Libra, C-bra. D-bra. G-bra. Alphabetically teats, we love you. We are with you. A woman's mind is the only place to be at night.

#27
Whenever you may feel you are loving your mind; just come
to me and I will help you love it completely.

#28 WRITING
Poets are dreamers. They dream of being poets. One
reason poetry is so fine (in my eyes) is because no one
ever reads it.

#29
Tuberous begonias on the whirlwinds of fame, flying like
rhinestones on the dawn's purple exit. Hurricane seasons
and typhoonite salt pepper the precepts of iodized fault. I
loved you when you were three, and I love you now that
you're one. Loving you is putting a round square into a
peg-hole, my body.

#30
Early morning words with warm catcher birds. Pushpin with
papers push them here and there and around the corners of
dusky rooms. I find probable answers for improbable questions. I make collections of things that I find; put them into
lines and remember them from one to eternity. This way they
will have a flow which is time to themselves. And they will be
true to me: the collector-arranger. It is the small objects that
infringe upon me.

#31

Yellow jonquils under the ochre ocean ply purplish sequins on paler potions. Timely squanders yonder maidens, wiggling scriggling liquid protein day dries to solid folded oceans. Tidled waves on the portions squarely marking tables' lotions (touching downy opening dollies, oily semen's soiling trolleys). Touching openly the crowded notions, opening doors on oily doilies seamen sealing soiled trolleys.

#32 WRITING

How I'd wish to be a poet. All words are magic, all utterances tragic. Collections of masterly stamps: blue Indians and tobacco leaves. Hundreds of the something placed in an order of disordered order. Odor and over and under asunder, as under the spreading chest stand smithy on graph paper of blue.

CHAPTER FIVE

#33 WRITING

Reference dictionary for valium or val-u-m, valley-m, val-lee-oom, va-lee-um, va-leum, va-laum, va-luem; a tablet pill making the user thinking of valium; introducing individuals of distinct maleness who are twenty-six with the overall impression of sixteen to twenty-one. Adolescent limbo in cages of stainless steel, hearing the rhythm without the bars. Never enabling themselves to dance with the tune. The cage is too small.

#34 TIME

You are a motherfucker turning this paper over. Maybe you're expecting some surprise. I ask you motherfucker, have you any idea that you're engaging in annihilating subversive activities by reading this? Don't go on with this! Stop where you are! (Fatherfucker.) Too many surprises

Danny Allen, India ink. 1973.
Collection of WTW.

like this may undermine your security. What would you do if the yellow lines in the road fade away? Would you pass any ongoing vehicle? Playing games with death is the only way to live.

#35 TIME
The egg-roll is gathering moss. The moisture of time is upon me. (What asks me for egg-roll than a surly Chinese cock.) Going for eastern than western, omelets are among the juiciest.

#36 LOVERS
When babies are born who have many mothers, how will the mother know how he is or if she is. Of course she knows. One more dream of David and the choir sings for me. A Christmas carol or is it a corral?

#37
China becomes the hypnosis of reality and the charmer of worldwide real estate. The estates must be broken and assimilated to make the new estate. And it will be painted red.

#38 TIME
It's almost 2000 in 1972. When it is 2000 everyone will see "2000 and 1." They will look at it thinking how much it's like how we see "Flash Gordon" now.

#39
Smoking grass makes me feel self-conscious because
I already do. To let those fears flee (when I'm high) makes
me so free. The joy is at one point unbearable and acute.
The peaks become sharper and the valleys greener.

#40 TRAVELING
We went to the East and turned the refrigerator up the
Arctic before leaving. Upon our return we opened the door
"and what to our wondering eyes did appear" but a penguin
(frozen) as was the cream cheese. Even Murray the Ape was
overwhelmed.

#41 WATER AND #48 PLATE
Eight inches of snow fall out of a print in your head onto a
ground of white lace. Could you find the millions of ice cubes
in every iceberg? Only by not looking for them. The doorway
to unconscious power faced with the mirror of your own lies.
And the reflection of a lie will not tell the truth. Maybe the ice
cubes will melt. Think how difficult then it would be to locate
water within water.

#42 GOLDEN NAILS
I guess we could have danced all night if I'd known you
would be there. Walking blindly I'd follow. There's only one
way to go. That is up or that is down. There's too much paper
to write non-deliberately. Even so, would you let me spend
days licking marbles off a chocolate plate? And relinquish my
long held belief that excel. Chiefly my interests sometimes
curve toward pounding golden nails into everything.

CHAPTER SIX

#43
A salami sandwich for a jazz fanatic. A buff for a rose, a kiss on the nose, and I'd like one now.

#44
Death probe, kill chose. Depth charge too shows. A stranger took a leap to the top of a park. Where those will leave a peck into cheese, and leave the haggard border hem.

#45 Traveling
Going down and around. "Over hill, over dale, as we hit the country trail." We found a town named Angelica. Angel-ice and angler for Spring trout. Trout springs traveling upstream, going our way underneath. The flow is not there, whence comes the eternal spring? Water, liquid and cold, refusing to be ice, saying way to the stoppage of winter's still guilt. Almost unbelievably, miraculously and definitely it is spring-time. The weather says now melt and grow.

#46
Yes in French is we in Swedish. Ja. I want to see the thing move without touching it. I know it will go. If will was enough we wouldn't have fingers. Until we do not have our fingers, there is no hope for moving matter with will power. We need some energy and a transference system to get the message from the sender to the doer. We need

some movers. From one human mind to another we can feel thought, and how do they come? Through the air? How could it be possible? Your brain is a sender and a receiver. A ghost is a ghost. And some live on sending thoughts to ourselves. If you're a receiver you know it. Let your mind tell you what you want to hear.

#47
On top in a smoke yard inside pinkish gates, soft and encrusting a pineapple waits for the cream whipped to mountains of peaks. Unders and elevator ties can walk over cross over the divide of skies. Knots for a dandy who catches a Sioux by the toe, to show the elation of licking a shoe.

#48 TIME
Make words stay together in a green tile or plate. Punch the clock and swear it's too late. When seconds tick into apricot orange they'll say "duck" if a goose flies by. (A duck whose mother is a buffalo hunter.) A gun for the Indian cannot kill a skyscraper.

Danny Allen, watercolor, 1972. Collection of WTW.

#49

Wake of the red ships washing abounds. In glee told me
the size of the sun. They said measure your ivory tureen.
Cranberries in sausage with a steaming dish of yogurt
culture, both punctured with steak knives. Feel it when it
will refine to stale sweet roles. On the style of edges they
asked "would you please not be so exacting?" This thing
is cold and its sides need sanding and impending. Would
you see the rounds becoming sounds? In silence they
wander for Simon the Pie man. The first view of summer
comes in late winter snowflakes. They're dampened in cones
on loan from the friendlier neighborhood. Bears beware
of yellow stones and rocks with moss. They would gather
reflections of mass only moss. The heart of a wanderer
has edges running into the other and becoming round in
the dusky light. You may see, but it is not there. A memory
of the sun being moon on the Earth.

#50
No entity shall envelop this being this ego of mine. It has a spine and it will never break but a tender word will have it bend. A funeral for fear in a casket of fawning bitches in blue tights. Go to Hell and stay in Hades. I know you and will not know you. You never were the protector you're made out to be. You belong in the soup. Did you know I cook your soup in the toilet?

#51 Blue
In the spring of the conscious mind of man, under willow's weeping, timing their winds for spaciousness, sounding whipper's will sprinkling drops. The semen of God is multiplied five thousand fold of loaves and fishes for worms and mushrooms. Lay me on the wettened ground the resounding sound of trees whispering to themselves. Their trunks grow to heaven of skies and reply I am blue. Penchants of pendants; demagogues resigned from their postcards of paper. Their sorrowful frowns go farther than time. Their eyes see no other than inside their rhymes. Ghosts of brown orchids and creases of dust on the boards.

CHAPTER SEVEN

#52
Time has the overabundance of waiting. In garbage cans and floated fans of childish trimmings; on lawns of distaste and reflectors streaming red. As the sun sets on sand dunes and blossoming wine. On the vine in the rain of a glistening grape. A porridge of raisins grows wild in an orchard of sunspots and freckles of anxiety. Let it out, let it find the gravity of its own mind. Unaired a hurricane of disastrous destiny. Check each play of the pen. Step back and let it out again.

#53

Immediate responses to questions never asked: reeling around in my mind. Could it write forever? There seems to be an overflow that needs a place to roam: a plateau of vengeance reading "no vacancy." No one knows where travels end that have no direction except what came before: knowing you will be going but not knowing when or where. Say "go" by feeling the instinct alone. It is the guide of sincerity because it has no goal but change.

#54

When it's time to eat chicken you know you're over twenty-five in body, mind and spirit. Chicken is fine fried so get the gasses burning. Hot vapor from a tongue of boiling water. The pot never boils if it is watched too closely; so pay no attention and it will do the inevitable. They put what's to cook inside. I love my lobster hot and juicy.

#55

I love words because they follow each other on a two-dimensional surface. The letters in each word are connected and the letters of all words are connected by white spaces. I will be a poet of words and of mind images. (I spent time trying to separate the two, but now will bring them together where they are and always have been.) I was denying writing for the things I love most.

#56

Could touching be lies? When a boy wants your love what do you feel? Okay. You will fall in a gray hole of sparkling light. Love him, he demands your love. Here it is. (It is lies.) Are you positive about what you're saying? No. (And it is lies.)

How could it be that you tell lies when you say no? Why would you say no if one is a lie? What you mean is yes. I am not afraid to make love to you. Give me your cock, or I'll put my dirty sock over your head. You'll be there: a thief in the

night. Your magic does not touch me. Please push the reject button, take off that stupid sock and zipper your fly. Because of my advice you just zippered your cock. I'll drop it on the wooden floor. Goodbye. I wonder how I will think of love now. At the end of this letter it won't be permitted not to say I love you.

#57

Each one of my objects is a gesture for your sake—for your existence to be what you need it to be. A child is a perfect creation. How would you feel if your painting was important and informed to go where you instructed? You would be nothing less than its father; opening doors and letting it go. So, whatever child opens a door? Do you need your own approval for doing what you're doing; or do you feel it is your existence that is your completion? Hi folks. I got your letter on white bark…The letters come from friends like sweet sounds of spring; and they bring a prelude of love and curiosity, and hope to be seeing each other again. Because you know that letters between friends may not go on forever. I'm writing sooner than it is possible, that your friend has not written a letter for many months. And more disheartening is the sound that you're not with your friend for longer.

#58

Why do we need this heavenly isolated universe to live in? Here the beauty of chance effects can most easily be appreciated because they are happening in an assembly that is control.

#59

Through unforgiving eyes of reality I see improved imaginary landscapes numbering in the ones of thousands. I want so badly to go back to that time when I did not mean to justify myself. When doing what I did and thinking my adult childhood thoughts were the reason for being alive. Today the reason is darkness; there is no reason. And this thought makes my life pleasurable and unbearable. I want the perfection of time and space that exists only in my mind. I believe I will live there.

#60
Arenas of area. Divas and Shivas. Holiness benders. The arrowroot enters and candlestick peters. Characteristics of many robed confessors, sin eaters. A man will give you the magic of realizing a fun-filled afterlife, without strife you desire a pleasant death. The instructions say: give over to death all the happiness of life, and you will be glad in death. The confessors have never seen God, nor heard God's word, nor felt God touch. Live this life with creation. You are part of it like the plants who grow upwards.

#61
I know where it is and ask to enter once again. The door has opened. There's no question that I will go there. She is there. My completion, my mother, my wife, my lady, my protector, my godmother: woman of perfections. She is the woman I know and need in one. A temptress and a grace. I am the caretaker of the gardens in our mind. She will know how to care and say no. Love is in these mingling waters, and their protective arms of shielding falls keep me in the darkened cave where no one enters except you.

#62
I'm writing for the maker of the Lord to reveal to me how he became the one to create the God who created me.

#63
Given the page and the number you'll choose a passion that's proper forever who's going to market to buy-a-pass. (O these chrome-plated names.) Aurora aura.

#64
When dawn, review the pink-spotted leaves for inspiring order. These words'll flow to you, least awaiting any inspiration and find you.

#65
I could not pass this loving cup if seeing you were looking up. Snowing seasons not in pain and loving you if you felt in vane. When ebbs of time adverse the flow, reverse the phase of moon tides show. In unlined faces wrinkling grow dear: how expensive the times are when changing the year. Soles for the fishes where water walks fast. But last and quite least death seals the past.

#66 [No entry]

#67
Red berries one sees on green powered branches of bushes, rushes of thyme and Hazelwood beaches. Sand dunes of sages as seen by the ages.

#68
I see squares on the ceiling. How or why should this be? Squared to their edges and looking at me. The disciplined contours reboarding the gloom of round-cornered pegs in a cube circled room.

#69
March on the idea in amber dawns, on the silvery line of unfolded pawns. Return the love of a tune's demise; each day to day unflickering lines.

#70
Snafu: in disorder, out of control, chaotic, muddle. From the initial letters of "situation normal, all fouled up."

#71
I love you Mr. Ginsberg. Would you do me, would you?
Would you blow the best cock of my generation? Hot cocks
are good with maple syrup and fried eggs. You freak in the
night, blow it.

#72
Once you catch her you may never let her go. If you were
from a chipmunk; this is the only stipulation in your life.
Rumor has it that a chipmunk lives his life so contentedly, in
bliss. One day ignorance flies as awareness arrives. He hears
himself say "I am a woodchuck." He is disillusioned with
self-awareness and kills himself. Self-destruction. "Dan? Hey
Dan!" "Yes what is it?" "Did you know…did you…I said Dan
did you know?" What did I know? She delivers a rhapsody in
blue for me and for you.

CHAPTER EIGHT

#73
The greatest fear is that I am becoming sicker, all the while
being in a delusion of becoming better. Where is the reality
I've heard so much about? Art is sometimes the great beauty
(pathos) produced by a crushed spirit in its struggle to re-
solve its death and be reborn. My son John: mice on John.
Flies fornicating on a girl's nose. Have I stayed too long at
the fair?

#74
Witch way to the left and then south, to the good, to the
bad. Glenda the good is melting yellow water monkeys. East
and west: bad. The tubular brigand cheering red and blue
maniacal finalities. North and south: good. Tapping her ruby
slippers on the day the apes said yes. Botticellian egg box,
pink banana. Thank you for the earth sun woman.

Danny Allen, watercolor, 1972. Collection of WTW.

#75
There's one place to go when you feel this low. Here on the
farm there is warmth in my arms. I know you can see the
hole of me: a light shining out of a window of doubt. A doorway for hope opens and closes. It swings on its hinges well
oiled and foreshorn. Though I'm owing no faith for the door
of my own, I'll kiss you and love you, and give you this home.

#76
Psycho-anal-yzed, psycho-anal eyezd, psycho-anal-eyesed.
Psycho-anal-eyes. A penis stuck in an eye cavity. Or, a penis
with an eye on its head looking into someone's asshole. Or,
doctor you are an asshole trying to fuck me.

#77

He flies from the nook and alights on the jar. Get out of my way you furry thing, cookies of cat words. She loves her stance, her romance and her stare. Her hot curly whiskers tell radial spaces of fours maimed by turns. Her shoe catches fire. Her nose blisters hot designing browned cookies of mincemeat and plot. There's no story line where these wild monsters grow. There's a time and a place for the pork chops to glow. At the time of the thyme it is six o'clock. Enough of these cookies, my intestines won't rot if you feed me some apples with lemon and lime.

#78

All the women I have friendships with I am in love with them like I was with my mother. And I am jealous of their mates like I was jealous of my father. She is my friend though, and I am safe being enshrined in fear of making love to her. And I am afraid of making love to my mother. And afraid of the women I love without a husband. But she has many boy-friends of the mind.

#79

We've been sewing: all day I've been showing him how to sew. His star is brightly shining and sows the seeds in me of generosity. We thread and rethread machines of delicate stares. Measuring tables in circles of blue and green squares.

CHAPTER NINE

#80

Rox with golden folds of hair, blue folds of silk. And perfect balance permeates all the folds. Thy roseated knockers: and there is one of them, the other rose is budding. She's lost her hands and her arms. She rests leaning slightly on the oxygen vapors. Unseen, clinging in there. Though is she waiting for Jim to be seen? Her blueness flows between her legs. They

will not open for this camera. Rox is in her house that is
not her house that is not her house. Eva lives there. And
Eva goes to lonelier deserts, leaving rocks for Jimmy, and a
gymnasium for Roxanne.

#81
A boy with velvet skin arrives escorted by a lady delivering
him into my unsafe soul. Is he the victim or are we? It was
yesterday, no this is romantic reverie. And why are events
now not calculable; there is no mathematics. We three held
each other one by one by me and united something of us;
unable to let go to raise the egg whites and give it all at ten
o'clock to the other man whom we love dearly but do not
embrace. For some unknown reason the distance between
us is closer than mere skin contact.

#82 [No entry]

#83
Chill, serve on lettuce. Chop finely, benignly, and wait now
forever. At last, the supper begins for the fast. But go slow,
and below there's a hairy feast. And a smile for my kinky
Jew. Ah love you granulated sugar. And curls over. Stop
now and let me come.

#84
It is a loving day today. Visitations and annunciations,
plague me in skin; touching the most intimate part of my
body, namely my brain. On some train. Bill made love to
me, I made love to Bill. Together we found the invisible line
between people and banished it. Diana made love
to me, I made love to Diana. She hungers for my penis and
wants it on finger terms. Tony talked about the invisible
line between people, and more so between artists, and we
banished it until he left. Steven suffered the lonely temperature of 102 degrees. And was it the look of love he hungered
for? Or the pain of a partner in sickness.

#85
So today so far I've smoked a pack of filter Marlboros and
they were pretty good. They were especially good when
someone else wanted one. And they weren't mine to give
so I gave them freely. Who's going to miss three cigarettes
when there's twenty boxes this week alone? And too many
microbes all over the world who desperately need a home.

#86
At times the smell of me exhaling a smoky cigarette and
putting it out is smelling like rabbit urine on old hay with
rabbit turds when I clean the rabbit's cages.

#87
Bob asks "if dogs run free why can't we?" And it is because
they will always come back to our cages of love. And we
know we will always let them go again. Some kind of faith
and it's okay being a dog.

#88
On the first warm day in May won't you come a calling and
bring me a sweet bouquet: So the sun shines in the clouds
of May and all the lovers are walking. Saying "love me" but
not in so many words. Really "one love": Indian talk from
the body of man to the body of man, in a circle going around
never ending always starting. I would give myself to every
body and be the great lover. To be in love though is where
we want to be.

#89
I know this dream is not going to end. I won't let it bend.
I won't let it rend, I won't let it break. I'm broken. And spat-
tered as grass on a mirror: a glass for rearview reflection.
Of time passing lightly on lawns of white ashes. Cremations
sublime, or a cow's utter ashes on Mama's brown eyes, and
the cow's lullabies.

#90
Butterflies of the eighteenth ridiculous on an amazing
degree of beatitude for a true-to-life escape into nonexistent
reality where we feel those coffee pangs if pain of empty
stomach blues. I concentrate on other's minds to let the
words come out on paper, and know what's going before
without reading the lines.

#91
I'm walking, I'm talking. I'm needing the ready: the electric
bill's too low. The heat's on slow. The fillet of sole's well
browned, the whale of shark's renowned for his spewing
of flashes of gasses. The water's ice cold. Run a wine to
the sperm whale. Thank God you have not a tale to tell the
electrician.

#92
There's no depths like the wrong depths when you're trying
to travel light. There is no wrong like the right wrong of the
blue song is not sung. And going to Mexico by way of Cairo.
For Acapulco is united. A corporation sings the song of
death for my whales.

#93
Now is the time for the holy incantations. Bring the goblet,
the crystals of water, the icings of love. This engagement is
ended. The part is not over, and dust turns to dust I would
want you in any form. I would believe you. I would love you.

#94
Reverential distance they are 4 ½ by 6 feet. They are different sizes depending on the viewers' site. This outsider ca-
thedral holds some holes of its own. The earth, the stones,
the grasses, the wind. The cream clothes on squared words.
Sun here is there and everywhere realizing the shape of
things undone.

Danny Allen, Conté crayon, 1973.
Collection of WTW.

DAN 73

#95

I sit and wonder if jelly beans would fly and I do want to
get closer to that boy. I'm still being loved by this woman
who loves me so much? Logic gets me nowhere this time. I
begin again. In this plane is a satisfaction to feed compulsive
infantile habits. I demand to be fed. And am fed every morsel
of intellect. To be castrated. To be hated. To be caged. To be
forced to create. To become the monk of monks. A numb
nun in denim. And I am loved for these things, and they are
never enough; but have me ever hungry for the other sides
of fences. Where I might see nothing in the God I know is
there, weighing exactly the balance of what I know in here.

THE EDGE OF GLASS
by Danny Allen

1.
The Edge of Glass, the dune, the ruin,
the edge of glass
The sharp edge of glass the edge of glass
The movement of the rising moon the orange moon.
The edge of glass.
The cold edge cutting a line in space
The water below.
The water show the edge of glass as a line
Cutting the water into sparkling slivers of glass.
The sky of indigo, of moon in the orange moon rising.
Above the slivers of water and the edge of glass,
the edge of glass.
The sand, the dune
The ruin
The endless, mindless ruin turns to sand.
And the water of glass of slivers of glass of
Splinters of glass cuts the moon.
The orange moon. The sand, the dune the ruin.
The sand
The edge of glass.

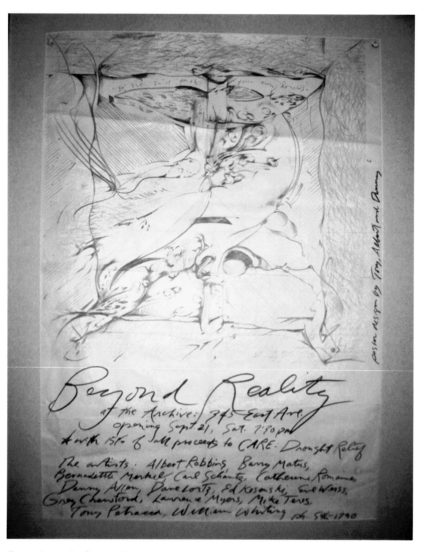

Poster design by Danny Allen, Antonio Petracca, and Albert Robbins.

2.
Garnish guarantees giant gobblers Tom turkeys to trees.
The turkeys to warlocks; tie ribbons in bows
Thanksgiving wishes:
November turns a season of summer in gold
To a turnstile of wanderers in the white solitude.
Sangria, meat of rabbits.
Unmerciful godlike mushrooms in a milky broth.

3.
The bats the birds.
The cats the turds.
The rats in herds.
The mate the innards.
The grate the cars the pats on words.
The hate the murders on rats on yards.

4.
The bat the bat upon the head.
The mouse any ouch, the cat say dog, the cheese
say please.
She had bat the cat upon the dog.
Her God say ouch, the mouse say house, the horse
say neigh.
The bore say nor.
The gas say high.
The vapor. The rich say poor or nor any bat. If she bat the
bat upon the bat.
She said the bat upon the seat.
The seat say bat the dog say God.
The God say cat.
The mouse say please.
The cheese say gas.
The vapor.

5.
Mainstream Main
Line say line say line saline.
Salt my malt say fault my line.
Say fine so fine so fine the stream the line
The running line the mine the way so stay.
So say the sale your salt my salt.
My salt Marie my sweet.
My mine my salt my scene my seen [mycaen] my
find my caen.
My line say fine reline refine remain.
Say line so find the stream the lines.

6.
So see the sea the see sees sea
The lan de vie the mer de vie.
The wave of sea the sea sees sea.
The row sees me the see seas saw
The saw sees wood.
The would would wood of sea would see would.
See wood see the skys.
The sail the wood.
The board would be the sea if it would see the sea.
It wood be the see.

7.
The day to day the daily diary daily.
Dog to dog (daily).
Dan say door.
Say day say dan say daily.
Say day say day say May say may.
Sa ami say Amy.
Say word say bird say should say naught.

Danny Allen. collage. paper. ca. 1970. Collection of WTW.

DAN 73

Danny Allen, two untitled drawings in Conté crayon, 1973.
Collection of Bill Root.

Danny Allen, color study for The Visitor, *acrylic on board.*
Collection of Wendy Lippman.

Danny Allen, collage, paper, ca. 1970. Collection of WTW.

Danny Allen. India ink. Collection of Susan Plunkett.

Bill Whiting is a vision-impaired artist, designer, and craftsman who produces intricately detailed artwork in spite of the challenges he faces with his eyesight. Bill has designed and executed large-scale murals for several hospitals, including Shriners Hospital for Children in Philadelphia, which landed him an appearance on the TODAY Show. Whiting has been the subject of two separate profiles on HGTV highlighting his skills as a painter and an architectural model builder. One of his elaborate dollhouses is in the permanent collection of the Toy and Miniature Museum of Kansas City.

Bill has illustrated a children's book, *Wings of Love*, and his artwork has appeared in various publications, including the *New York Times* and *Architectural Digest*. He has been featured in model-building publications, but he is best known for his presentation portraits of notable Philadelphians, with portraits hanging throughout the city, including historic Pennsylvania Hospital.

Bill Whiting currently lives in Philadelphia, Pennsylvania with his trusty Jack Russell terrier, Winifred P. Jumpingbean, who takes top billing in his weekly political-satire blog, *WinnieToons.com*. *An Early Work Late in Life* is his first book.

Bill Whiting with longtime friend and noted photographer, Eva Weiss, 2012.

Layout and design:
Katherine Denison
Denison Creative
www.denisoncreative.com

Production and printing:
pixelPRESERVE
www.pixelpreserve.net